Nanolaminate Predicated on Moiety Morphospatial Dielectric Aggregatum

Sereno M

Nanolaminate Predicated on Moiety Morphospatial Dielectric Aggregatum

First Edition October 2025

Written by Sereno M

CONTENTS

CHAPTERS

1

INTRODUCTION

1.1 WHAT IS FUNCTIONAL MATERIALS?

Functional materials are advanced materials engineered for specific purposes due to their unique intrinsic properties. They are widely used in electronic devices for applications such as magnetic, magnetocaloric, magnetoelastic, spintronic, optical, catalytic, thermometric, ferroelectric, piezoelectric, and dielectric functionalities. These materials play a key role in energy-efficient systems, sensing, energy conversion, actuation, and computation. One of their most remarkable features is tunability in response to external stimuli, including electromagnetic radiation, mechanical stress, temperature changes, magnetic fields, and electric fields. This responsiveness opens up a broad range of potential applications across technology and industry.

1.2 DIFFERENT CATEGORIES OF FUNCTIONAL MATERIALS AND THEIR APPLICATION

Functional materials can be divided into several categories:

- **Nanomaterials/nanoparticles**: Nanoparticles are extremely sensitive to external factors due to their large surface area, which facilitates surface interactions affected by temperature, pressure, light, and electric fields, making them useful in biomedical analysis, catalysis, photovoltaic, and light-emitting diode applications. Additionally, incorporating nanomaterials into a composite can enhance the mechanical, thermal, and electrical properties of an existing 'Functional material'.

- **Ceramics**: Ceramics are inorganic materials with high melting points and good mechanical and thermal properties. They are used in a variety of applications, such as refractories, construction materials, and biomedical implants. Examples of ceramics include alumina, zirconia, and silicon carbide.
- **Shape memory and rare earth based alloys**: These materials can recover their original shape after being deformed, making them useful in medical devices and actuators.
- **Composite**: These are made up of two or more different types of materials, which combine their individual properties to create a material with specific properties. Examples of composites include polymer, two-dimensional nanosheets, fibreglass, carbon fibre composites, and ceramic matrix composites.
- **Biomaterials**: Biomaterials are materials that interact with biological systems, either temporarily or permanently. They have applications in tissue engineering, drug delivery, and medical implants. Examples of biomaterials include hydrogels, collagen, and titanium alloys.
- **Two dimensional materials**:Graphene, hexagonal boron nitride (h-BN), borophene, phosphorene, MoS_2, $MoSe_2$, and MXENES are a few of the 2D materials that have gained significant attention due to their exceptional mechanical, optical, thermal and magnetic proprties [1–3]. These materials have exhibited immense potential in various fields such as sensing, flexible/low power electronics, spintronics, detector/emittor, super-capacitor, battery and water purification applications.
- **Topological Materials**: Topological insulators such as Bi_2Se_3, Bi_2Te_3, and Sb_2Te_3 have high thermoelectric performance [4], making them ideal for energy conversion and low-dissipation switching devices. They can also be used for novel applications such as spin-orbit torque memory, spintronics, spin filter, quantum computing, and low-dissipation circuit design [5, 6]. Weyl semimetals exhibit exotic electronic properties

like chiral anomaly and negative magnetoresistance, with potential applications in electronics, spintronics, and photonics.

1.3 NEED FOR NEW NOVEL FUNCTIONAL MATERIALS

The demand for better, faster, and smart devices in industry and consumer markets has led to the pursuit of alternative, energy-efficient, and multi-functional materials and device structures. Traditional semiconductor technology relies heavily on magnetic metals, and conductive polymers, which have limitations in terms of density, environmental stability, and high-cost of fabrication techniques. Novel functional materials like carbon nanomaterials, graphene, transition metal dichalcogenides (TMDs), metal-organic framework, perovskite materials and smart polymers offer a wide array of applications.

A recent addition to the family of novel functional materials is two-dimensional (2D) materials with potential application in electronic, optoelectronic, and spintronic devices for their ultra-thin body, light-matter solid interactions, and compatibility with CMOS technology. Additionally, the robust mechanical properties of 2D materials make them ideal compared to bulk and thin film devices for fabricating portable and flexible wearable devices. The advantage of such novel devices is that they have high real-time accuracy and are resistant to damage, which can revolutionize the industry. Therefore, the discovery of these novel functional materials will enable us to fabricate unique devices for various applications such as motion detection, textiles with intelligent features, sports activity monitoring, health monitoring and flexible robotics.

Throughout my doctoral research, I have permormed extensive theoretical and experimental work on functional materials, with a primary emphasis on two-dimensional, topological, and composite materials. My experimental work involved the study of the magnetic and transport properties of magnetic topological insulator systems, as well the investigation of resistive switching properties of composite systems. Additionally, I have utilized first-principles-based Density Functional Theory to study the electronic, magnetic, optical, and transport properties of various 2D materials like phosphorene, Bi_2Se_3, $CrGeTe_3$, and $MnBi_2Te_4$, along with their potential applications. In the forthcoming sections, I will provide a concise overview of 2D materials, topological insulators, magnetic topological insulators, and their respective applications.

1.4 TWO DIMENSIONAL MATERIALS

The physical dimension of the system plays a huge role in influencing its physical and chemical properties. In 2D materials, one of the dimensions lies in the nanometer range, which makes them highly sensitive to external factors and thus has a high surface-to-volume ratio. At low dimension, dominating quantum mechanical effects causes various intriguing phenomena like the Quantum Hall effect, topological edge state, Van Hove singularity, Dirac fermions, Valleytronics etc [7–9].

There are various techniques to synthesize two-dimensional (2D) materials, such as Chemical vapour deposition (CVD), Physical vapour deposition (PVD) techniques like molecular beam epitaxy, atomic layer deposition, RF/DC sputtering and mechanical/sonochemical/liquid phase exfoliation of Van der Waals materials.

2D and Van der Waals (vdW) materials are closely related but not entirely similar. While 2D materials are systems having one of the dimensions squeezed to the nanoscale and the atoms arranged in a crystal lattice characterized by strong intralayer bonding, vdW materials result from the stacking of such two-dimensional (2D) layers that are bounded in the third dimension through a weak, non-covalent interaction known as van der Waals forces. The weak vdW force between the layers allows them to exfoliate easily into thin layers. I will briefly discuss the Van der Waals materials in the next section.

1.4.0.1 VAN DER WAALS MATERIALS

In the 16 years since Novoselov and Geim [10] isolated a single layer of graphite, graphene, the scientific area of 2D Van der Waals materials has blossomed to embrace various types of nanosheets of single or multiple atomic species. The atomic-level structure of Van der Waals materials is characterized by strong intralayer covalent bonds that firmly hold atoms within each layer. At the same time, weak interlayer van der Waals forces maintain the vertical alignment of the layers. As a result, these materials can be cleaved layer by layer without affecting their atomic-level structural integrity. This unique property creates the test beds for investigating low-dimensional physics and designing heterostructures with diverse applications, including field-effect transistors, optoelectronics, and sensors.

1.5 WHY ARE 2D MATERIALS DIFFERENT FROM BULK MATERIALS?

- **Elimination of van der Waals interactions:** Strong intralayer covalent bonds keep individual layers together, while weak interlayer van der Waals forces hold the layers vertically. This allows for layer-by-layer cleaving while maintaining atomic-level structural integrity, resulting in exceptional electrical and optical characteristics perpendicular to the basal plane that is missing in their bulk crystals.

- **Increase in the surface area-to-volume ratio:** An increase in the surface area-to-volume ratio makes 2D materials extremely sensitive to external stimuli such as electromagnetic field, chemicals, light, and heat and allows for tailoring of their optical transparency, mechanical flexibility, and electrical properties.

- **Dangling bond-free surface:** Dangling bond-free surface makes 2D materials mechanically strong and simple to integrate with functional features like cavities and photonic crystals. Additionally, it allows for the fabrication of Van der Waals or twisted moiré heterostructures, offering a novel approach for atomic interface design, band engineering, and crystal symmetry control.

- **Quantum confinement effect:** Quantum confinement effect, resulting from the loss of periodicity perpendicular to the basal plane, affects the band structure and density of states of the material, accounting for unprecedented conductivity of materials like graphene.

However, all these fascinating properties can only manifest when high-quality materials and highly sophisticated and precise control to integrate them with the electronic circuit, and eventual commercialization necessitates large-scale synthetic processes are available.

1.6 OVERVIEW OF 2D MATERIALS SYNTHESIS

Synthesis tactics for two dimensional materials are broadly classified into two types: top-down approaches and bottom-up method.

1.6.1 TOP-DOWN METHOD

The top-down method uses chemical vapour transport (CVT) or flux growth to create ultrathin nanosheets. To isolate atomically thin flakes' mechanical exfoliation, ultrasonic wave and ion-exchange method is used. We used the micromechanical exfoliation technique for the purpose of exfoliating various Van der Waals materials, including $MnBi_2Te_4$, to be prepare suitable flakes for Transmission Electron Microscopy imaging.

- **Micromechanical exfoliation**: A stamp material, such as scotch tape, is used to cleave the flake from a crystal by applying a peeling force to the single- or few-atom-thick sheets .
- **Ultrasonic exfoliation**: This process uses high-frequency sound waves to break apart the bonds between the layers of the material, resulting in individual sheets that can be easily dispersed in solvents.

1.6.2 BOTTOM-UP METHODS

In bottom-up methods, atoms are directly assembled on the substrate to form ultra-thin high-quality nanosheets. Some of the bottom-up methods are Hydro/solvothermal synthesis, Microwave synthesis, Chemical vapour deposition and Physical vapour deposition.

1.7 EMERGING CLASSES OF 2D MATERIALS

There are several classes of 2D materials, including:

1.7 EMERGING CLASSES OF 2D MATERIALS

1.7.1 SINGLE ELEMENT ALLETROPES

The most widely recognized single-element 2D material is graphene, which consists of a single layer of carbon atoms arranged in a honeycomb lattice. Borophene, stanene, arsenene, germenene and other single elemental 2D materials have also emerged as promising candidates for various applications due to their unique properties, such as tunable bandgaps and high carrier mobility. For example, borophene, a monolayer of boron atoms, exhibited exceptional mechanical strength and tunable electronic properties, making it a potential candidate for use in nanoelectronics and flexible electronics. Similarly, promising results have been found for the topological insulator stanene, which is a single layer of tin atoms and has potential uses in spintronics and quantum computing.

Phosphorene is another single elemental 2D material that has attracted significant attention due to its unique properties. Phosphorene is monolayer of phosphorus atoms arranged in a honeycomb lattice. It was first theoretically predicted in 2014 by researchers at the University of Oxford, and later synthesized in the same year by researchers at the University of Michigan. It exhibits a tunable bandgap, high carrier mobility, and exceptional thermal and mechanical properties, making it a promising candidate for various applications, including electronics, optoelectronics, and energy storage. Phosphorene exhibits a direct bandgap which is maintained even as the number of layers changes. This property enables tunable and efficient light emission and absorption, rendering phosphorene a promising contender for use in optoelectronic devices. Additionally, phosphorene's highly anisotropic nature makes it it a promising candidate for use in electronic and optoelectronic devices. Till now, phosphorene has shown promising results as an anode material in lithium-ion batteries, due to its high theoretical capacity and excellent cycling stability. As research continues to uncover the properties and potential applications of phosphorene and other single elemental 2D materials, their impact on the fields of science and technology is expected to be significant.

One of the challenges of working with phosphorene is that it is not as stable as graphene or other two-dimensional materials. It can react with air and water, leading to oxidation and degradation. Researchers have found several ways to stabilize phosphorene, such as encapsulating it in protective layers or developing new synthesis methods. Despite the challenges, there is significant interest in the potential applications of phosphorene. Researchers are exploring its use in fields such as energy storage, catalysis, and biomedical engineering.

1.7.2 MXENES

MXenes are derived from layered carbides, nitrides, or carbonitrides known as MAX phases, which are exfoliated through selective etching, intercalation, electrochemical exfoliation and solvent exfoliation methods. MXenes are notable for their excellent chemical stability, high electrical conductivity, mechanical strength, making them ideal candidates for use in energy storage devices, catalysis, sensors, and other applications. Some examples of MXenes include Ti_2C, Ti_4N_3, and $Mo_2Ti_2C_3$.

1.7.3 2D OXIDES

Graphene oxide, Molybdenum oxide, Tungsten oxide, Zinc oxide etc., are popular 2D oxide materials due to their high reactivity, and excellent mechanical flexibility,.

1.7.4 2D MAGNETIC MATERIALS

Magnetic materials are distinguished from disordered systems by an ordered arrangement of the magnetic moments over long distances, leading to spontaneous time-reversal symmetry breaking. The exchange bias interaction between neighbouring magnetic atoms gives rise to ferromagnetism, anti ferromagnetism and ferrimagnetism in 3D systems. However, the Mermin-Wagner theorem [11] says that 2D magnetic materials cannot exhibit long-range order at any non-zero temperature due to the effects of these thermal fluctuations in a strictly 2D isotropic Heisenberg system. On the other hand, an easy-axis anisotropy might violate the rotational symmetry and sustain ferromagnetic order in 2D.

Therefore, the first experimental verification of exfoliated two-dimensional magnetic material chromium triiodide (CrI_3) in 2017 was a huge landmark in the scientific community. CrI_3 has a honeycomb lattice structure with layers that can be easily separated. In the bulk form of CrI_3, the magnetic moments of individual chromium atoms are coupled ferromagnetically within the layers and antiferromagnetically between the layers. Shortly after the discovery of CrI_3 [12], $CrGeTe_3$ (CGT) [13] was also successfully exfoliated to the monolayer limit. CGT is a tri-chalcogenide and has a hexagonal lattice structure in which six nearby Te atoms surround each Cr atom, and each of the two Ge atoms, oriented along the z-axis, is surrounded by three Te atoms. Interestingly, at its ground state, a single layer of CGT possesses ferromagnetic (FM) semiconductor characteristics with a typical indirect bandgap of 0.26 eV near the K point. The spin-up electronic state is 0.27 eV below the spin-down electronic state. Below we provide a brief overview of the common types of magnetic states in these materials (Table. 1.1)

Table 1.1: summary of two dimensional magnetic materials

	Chalcogenides	**Dihalides**	**Trihalides**
Ferromagnetic	$CrXTe_3$ (X = Si/Ge)[Cr^{3+}($3d^3$)]	–	CrX_3 (X = Br/I) [Cr^{3+} ($3d^3$)]
Ferromagnetic (itinerant)	Fe_3GeTe_2 [Fe^{2+}($3d^6$) and Fe^{3+}($3d^5$)] Fe_xTaS_2 (Fe intercalated)	–	–
Antiferromagnetic (A-type)	$MnBi_2Te_4$ [Mn^{2+}($3d^5$)]	FeX_2 (X = Cl/Br) [Fe^{2+}($3d^6$)]	$CrCl_3$[Cr^{3+} ($3d^3$)]
Antiferromagntic (C-type and G-type)	$MnPX_3$ (X = S/Se) (AF-Neel) [Mn^{2+} ($3d^5$)] MPS_3 (M = Fe/Co/Ni) (AF-zigzag) [Fe^{2+} ($3d^6$), Co^{2+} ($3d^7$) and Ni^{2+} ($3d^8$)]	–	–
Helimagnets	-	NiX_2 (X = Br/I) [Ni_{2+}($3d^8$)] – MnI_2 and CoI_2 [Mn^{2+}($3d^5$); Co^{2+}($3d^7$)]	-
Magnetoelectrics and multiferroics	MnPX3 (X = S/Se) (magnetoelectrics)	FeX_2 (X = Cl/Br) (magnetoelectrics) NiX_2 (X = Br/I) (multiferroics) MnI_2 and CoI_2 (multiferroics)	$CrCl_3$[Cr^{3+} ($3d^3$)] (magnetoelectrics)
Frustrated magnets	–	VX_2 (X = Cl/Br) [V^{2+}($3d^3$)]	$RuCl_3$ [Ru^{3+}($4d^5$)]

It has been observed that the spin and orbital angular momenta of 3d electrons in transition metal cations are the source of magnetic moments of magnetic Van der Waals materials. Long-range magnetic ordering is primarily driven by intralayer exchange interactions, as direct exchange interaction between magnetic ions is weak due to large cation-cation distances. However, the dominant interaction channel is the super-exchange interaction, mediated by non-magnetic anions between magnetic cations due to the crystal field splitting of the five 3d orbitals into three low-energy t_{2g} levels and two high-energy e_g levels from octahedral coordination of transition metal cations.

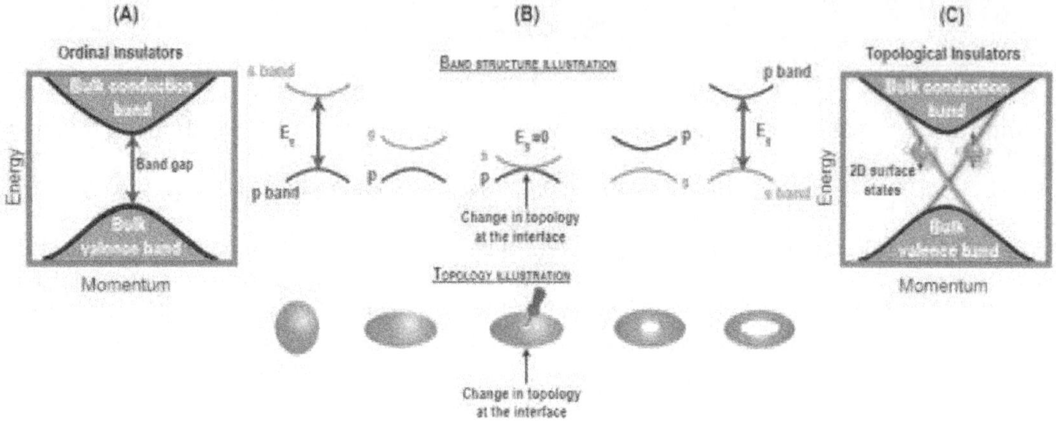

Figure 1.1: (A) Illustration of the bandstructure of a normal insulator. (B) Illustration of change in topology in the bandstructure from an ordinary insulator to a topological insulator. There is a topological change in the band structure at the interface, and due to the strong spin-orbit coupling in the TI material: the band order is reversed at the TI side. Similarly, a topological change takes place when coming from a sphere to a torus. (C) Illustrative band structure of ideal three-dimensional TIs with 2D surface states with spin up and down crossing from bulk valence band to bulk conduction band.

Experimental applications of two-dimensional magnetic materials include their use in magnetic sensing, spin filtering, and as building blocks for novel magnetic structures such as skyrmions. For example, CrI_3 has been used as a platform for magnetic sensing due to its high sensitivity to magnetic fields.

1.7.5 TOPOLOGICAL INSULATORS

A topological insulator (TI) has electrically conducting surface states but an insulating bulk state. These materials have spin-polarized surface states, meaning the spin direction of surface electrons is interlinked with their direction of motion. Due to the absence of backscattering states, spin-flip of an electron is prohibited, resulting in nearly dissipationless surface transport, even in the presence of non-magnetic impurities.

The emergence of metallic surface/edge states is a outcome of strong spin-orbit coupling (SOC) in the material, thus causing a band inversion. Spin-orbit coupling in materials with different orbital characters between the conduction and valence bands requires bandgap closure at the interface before deforming the band structure to the non-inverted form and reopening it with a reversed sign of the effective band mass. Topological and normal insulators (e.g., a vacuum) possess contrasting topological features in their band structures. Consequently,

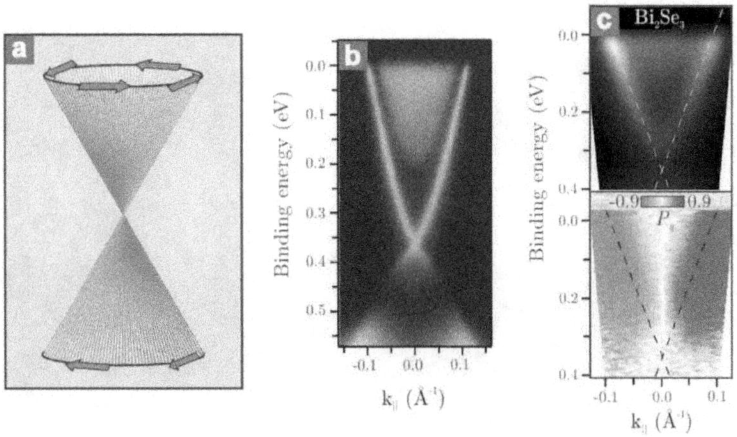

Figure 1.2: Spin helicity in exotic band structure of topological insulators. (a) Helical Dirac cone at zero magnetic field of an ideal TI. Backscattering is not allowed in such a system. (b) Experimental angle-resolved photoemission spectroscopy spectra of the 3D TI Bi2Te3. The linear surface bands are clearly resolved. However, the Dirac point is shadowed by bulk valence band states (Adapted from [14]). (c) ARPES spectrum of Bi_2Se_3 (top) with visible Dirac point and the corresponding (below) spin-polarized spectrum showing the helicity of the surface states. Color denotes the spin–polarization in y–direction. (Adapted from [15]).

forming an interface between the two leads to a closure and reopening of the bandgap as one transitions from the insulator to the TI regime. This change in topology, analogous to cutting a hole in a sphere, induces a metallic state at the interface (See Figure 1.1).

CdTe/HgTe/CdTe quantum wells were the first experimentally demonstrated 2D topological insulator system with counter-propagating spin-polarized conduction edge channels, exhibiting the quantum spin Hall effect. These channels were protected by time-reversal symmetry. Theoretically, 2D TI systems are characterized by the time-reversal invariant $\boldsymbol{Z_2}$, which can either be zero (trivial insulator) or 1 (topological insulator). The first 3D topological insulator was discovered in alloy Bi_xSb_{1-x} in 2007 by a team of researchers led by M. Zahid Hasan at Princeton University, where they mapped the unusual surface bands by angle-resolved photoemission spectroscopy (ARPES) measurement. 3D topological insulators that obey time-reversal symmetry are described by four topological $\boldsymbol{Z_2}$ invariants. As each invariant can adopt a value of either 0 or 1, a total of 16 categories of trivial and topological insulators exist.

The unique surface states of topological insulators could provide a platform for efficient spin manipulation and transport, making them ideal for next-generation electronics like spin-orbit torque-based switching devices. The robust surface states of topological insulators

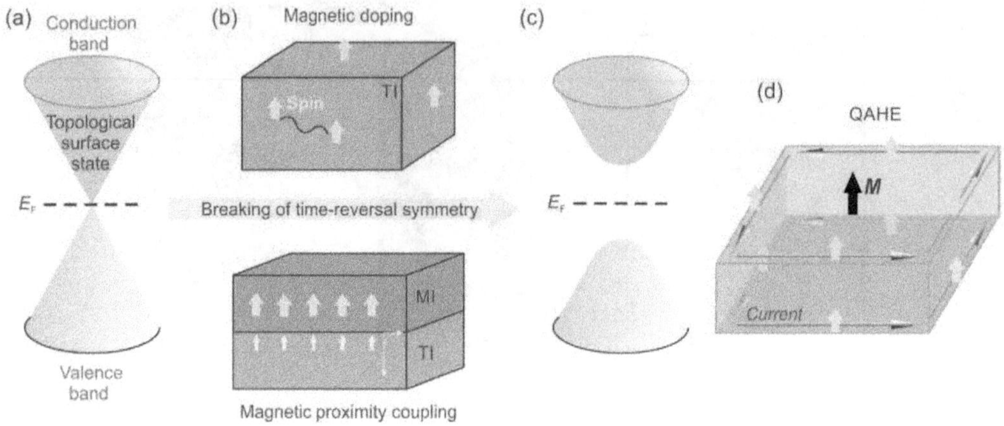

Figure 1.3: (a) Dirac cone band structure of topological insulators, (b) Broken time reversal symmetry in the presence of magnetic atom doping or magnetic proximity effect. c) Magnetic order resulting gapped surface state with Fermi level lying inside the gap. (d) Quantized conduction at both the upper and lower surfaces of a film, with the spin orientation parallel to the momentum direction.

could provide a stable environment for the fault-tolerant topological quantum computing, manipulation, and storage of quantum information. The strong coupling between the surface and bulk states of topological insulators could enhance thermoelectric performance. Additionally, topological insulators could be used as highly sensitive sensors and detectors for various applications, including magnetic field sensing, chemical sensing, and bio-sensing.

1.7.6 MAGNETIC TOPOLOGICAL INSULATORS

Magnetic topological insulators (MTIs) combine the properties of topological insulators and ferromagnets, leading to exotic electronic states like the quantum anomalous Hall effect (QAHE). Unlike other quantum Hall effects, the QAHE occurs without needing an external magnetic field and is more robust against disorder. MTIs provide a platform to observe the QAHE at higher temperatures, potentially developing new spintronic devices and topological quantum computers. MTIs also exhibits the magnetic proximity effect, wherein the electronic characteristics of the topological insulator can be modulated by the magnetic properties of the ferromagnet. This phenomenon offers novel opportunities for developing spin-dependent electronic devices.

1.7.6.1 DOPED MAGNETIC TOPOLOGICAL INSULATORS

Inspired by diluted magnetic semiconductors, Magnetism was introduced in the topological insulator system by doping them with 3d transition metal elements. The first experimental validation of the quantization of the Hall resistance ($\rho_{yx} = \frac{h}{e^2}$) was observed in a 5 nanometer thick Cr-doped $(Bi_{1-y}Sb_y)_2Te_3$ on a $SrTiO_3$ substrate. Since the quantization was observed to occur without any accompanying external magnetic field, the phenomenon has been identified as the QAHE. The longitudinal hall resistivity ρ_{yx} value ranges from $+\frac{h}{e^2}$ and $-\frac{h}{e^2}$ depending on the magnetic field direction.

1.7.6.2 TI/FMI HETEROSTRUCTURES

A surface exchange gap can be achieved through proximity coupling of topological insulators and ferromagnetic insulators. Unlike doping, this method avoids introducing lattice disorders. The exchange interaction is limited to the magnetic proximity effect at the interface, resulting in an insulating magnetic state on the surface. At a temperature of 400K, the $Bi_xSb_{(1-x)2}Te_3/Tm_3Fe_5O_{12}$ hetero-structure was observed to exhibit ferromagnetism without destroying the topological insulator surface state, which was evidenced by the clear presence of square shaped hysteresis loops. This robust ferromagnetism was found to result in a significant enhancement of the high-T_c behavior.

The realization of an antiferromagnetic topological insulator can be accomplished through the utilization of van der Waals magnets, which allow for the full manifestation of its layer-wise properties. Through the alternating arrangement of these layers in van der Waals hetero-structures, it becomes possible to integrate both topological properties and long-range magnetic order into a single material. Consequently, intrinsic magnetic topological insulators can be produced without the need for further doping or surface modifications.

1.7.6.3 INTRINSIC MAGNETIC TOPOLOGICAL INSULATORS

The pursuit of finding an intrinsic magnetic topological insulator has been eased by the confirmation, through both experimental and theoretical means, of A-type antiferromagnetic

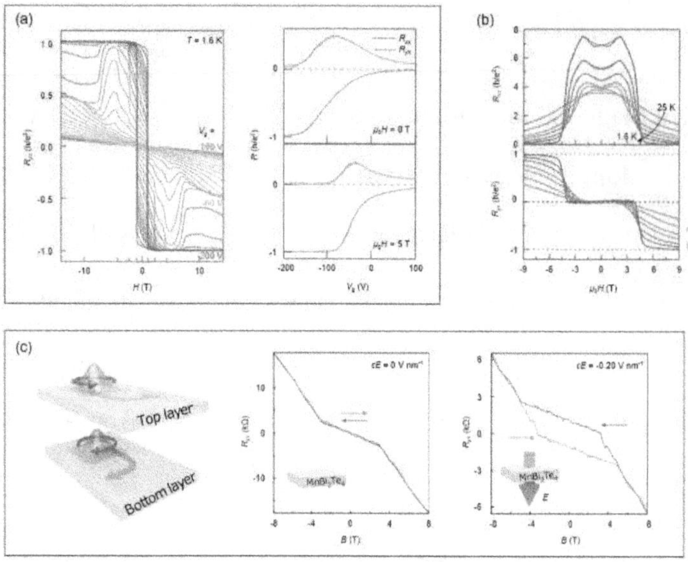

Figure 1.4: (a) Yang *et al.* showed the quantum anomalous Hall effect in a 5 septuple layer $MnBi_2Te_4$ device at T = 1.6 K, seen in Hall resistance vs. gate voltages and magnetic fields (Adapted from [17]). (b) Liu *et al.* observed a zero plateau in Hall resistance with magnetic field and gate voltage of 25 V (Adapted from [18]). (c) Gao *et al.* illustrated layer Hall effect in a 6-SL device with opposite deflections in top and bottom layers, and showed Hall resistances as a function of magnetic field at zero and finite electric fields (Adapted from [16]).

topological insulator $MnBi_2Te_4$ (MBT). In MBT, ferromagnetic coupling exists within each septuple layer (SL), while antiferromagnetic coupling exists between SLs. QAHE was observed in a 5-SL MBT device at 1.4 K, with the Hall resistance R_{yx} at $0.97\frac{h}{e^2}$ and longitudinal resistance R_{xx} at approximately $0.061\frac{h}{e^2}$ for magnetic field B = 0, as illustrated in Figure. 1.4. The Hall plateau at $0.998\frac{h}{e^2}$ was achieved for B > 2.5 T. In 6-SL MBT devices, a zero Hall plateau and high longitudinal resistance were reported, indicating an axion insulator state. The Hall voltage remained at zero under a gate voltage ranging from 22 V to 30 V for -3.5 T < B < 3.5 T, while the associated R_{xx} could increase up to $7.5\frac{h}{e^2}$ [16].

1.8 RECENT PROGRESS IN 2D MATERIALS

Creating van der Waals heterostructures is the natural next step in the advancement of 2D materials research following the exfoliation of single or bilayer materials. In the following section, I will discuss the recent development in Van der Waals heterostructure with a focus on 2D magnetic and topological material heterostructure.

1.8.1 VAN DER WAALS HETEROSTRUCTURE

The vdW heterostructures are composed of different monolayers stacked together, enabling the exploration of their unique properties. These heterostructures have opened up new possibilities in materials science, as the resulting structures can exhibit properties missing in the constituent layers alone. For instance, the encapsulated graphene with hexagonal boron nitride can protect the graphene from moisture or oxidation, leading to an extraordinary carrier mobility exceeding 10^6 $cm^2V^{-1}s^{-1}$.

Furthermore, vdW heterostructures (vdWHs) of transition metal dichalcogenides (TMDs) have demonstrated unique properties. For example, MoS_2–WSe_2 heterostructures exhibit an ultrafast hole transfer rate of around 40 femtoseconds [19], while $MoSe_2$–WSe_2 and $MoSe_2$–WS_2 systems show degenerate exciton charge transfer. vdWHs' carrier lifetimes matched or surpassed associated monolayers. Till date, MoS_2 devices with top-graphene contacts show notable Hall mobility up to 34,000 $cm^2V^{-1}s^{-1}$ and Shubnikov de Haas oscillations.

Magnetic vdW heterostructures may unveil novel phenomena like topological spin textures, Dzyaloshinskii-Moriya (DM) interaction at the interface. Recent calculations on $MnBi_2Te_4/CrI_3$ show potential for achieving the electrically tunable QAHE effect. Experiments have observed Né el-type magnetic skyrmions and topological Hall effect in Fe_3GeTe_2/WTe_2.

1.8.2 TWISTED HETEROSTRUCTURES

Twistronics occurs in misaligned bilayer or trilayer structures of 2D materials when a moiré pattern forms due to lattice mismatch and twist angle. This pattern creates a periodic potential modulation that alters the electronic properties, leading to the emergence of new electronic states. The twist angle affects interlayer coupling strength, degree of charge transfer, and the moiré superlattice, giving rise to nontrivial topology, strong electron-phonon coupling, flat bands and enhanced correlations.

Bistritzer and Macdonald predicted in 2011 at a twist angle, $\theta_r = 1.05°$ twisted bilayer graphene (TBLG) would exhibit flat band structure near the Fermi and in 2018 by Cao *et*

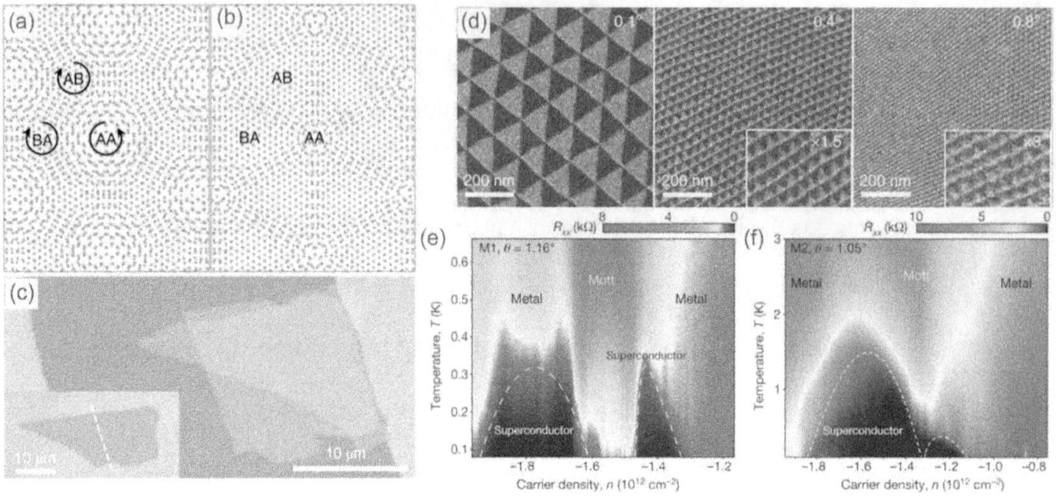

Figure 1.5: (a),(b) Schematic diagrams of the moiré superlattice c) Optical micrograph. d) Several TEM dark-field images for distinct twist angles.(Figure taken from [20]). (e) Metallic, Mott and superconducting state obsrved in a twisted bilayer graphene with θ_r=1.16°, (f) Disappearenece of superconductivity for θ_r=1.05°. Measurements performed at T = 1.7K. (Figure taken from [21])

al.[21] experiemntally demonstrated unconventional superconducting and magneto-transport properties TBLG for θ_r = 1.1°. Additionally, Cao *et al.*[22] demonstrated that the electric field can tune the superconductivity in alternating-twisted magic-angle tri-layer graphene twisted bilayer graphene. So, this demonstrates that moiré superlatice generated by the twist, can show unique quantum phenomena which is not an intrinsic property of the individul layer. Even at a larger twist angle of 30°, TBLG exhibited unique phenomena such as quasicrystal-like symmetry [23]. The scientific community has adopted the term 'Twistronics' to describe the study of the impact of twist angles on the electronic, optical and magnetic properties of stacked Van der Waals heterostructures.

Scientists have been studying Twistronics in heterobilayer structures such as graphene, h-BN, TMDs, and Janus materials. Experiments with $MoSe_2/WSe_2$ twisted heterobilayers showed a variation in average moiré exciton potential depth and twist angle. In WSe_2/WS_2 heterobilayers, the energy of the twist-angle-dependent exciton shifts continuously as the twist angle varies. Similar findings have been observed in MoS_2/WSe_2, $MoSe_2/WS_2$, and twisted bilayer MoS_2. [24–28]

Scientists are investigating "Twistronics" in various heterobilayer structures comprising graphene, h-BN, TMDs, and Janus materials. Forexample in WSe_2/WS_2 heterobilayers exciton energy shifted from 1.35 eV 1.57 eV. The correlation between θ_r and the photoluminescence spectra has been demonstrated in various heterobilayer configurations, such as MoS_2/WSe_2, $MoSe_2/WS_2$, and twisted bilayer MoS_2. [24–28].

1.9 APPLICATIONS OF 2D MATERIALS

2D materials, owing to their reduced dimensionality, exhibit distinctive characteristics that render them appropriate for several applications where conventional bulk materials are unsuitable. Below are some of the most encouraging applications.

ULTRA-THIN 2D PLANAR AND VERTICAL TRANSISTORS

2D semiconductor, specifically transition metal dichalogenides, are being extensively studied as potential channel materials for ultrathin transistors. In few-layer phosphorene FETs, electrons exhibited a field effect mobility of about 38 cm^2/Vs and holes showed a value of approximately 172 cm^2/Vs [29]. Meanwhile, few-layer MoS_2 transistors exhibited an intrinsic cut-off frequency of 42 GHz and a maximum power-gain frequency of 50 GHz[30].

SENSORS:

2D materials have been found to be highly suitable for gas, medical, disease, and toxic material sensing applications due to their high surface-to-volume ratio and ultra sensitivity to surface interactions [31]. Graphene-based sensors have shown remarkable sensitivity to gases such as nitrogen oxides, carbon monoxide, and ammonia, while transition metal dichalcogenides (TMDs) have demonstrated potential as biosensors due to their strong interaction with biological molecules [32]. The integration of these materials into sensing devices such as field-effect transistors (FETs) has offered excellent sensitivity and response time. For instance, WS_2-based FETs have been utilized for sensing ethanol and NH_3, and have exhibited elevated electron mobility of 12 $cm^2V^{-1}s^{-1}$ upon adsorption [33].

Similarly, $MoSe_2$ has shown unprecendented sensitivity of 300 ppm , mobility of 65.6 $cm^2V^{-1}s^{-1}$, instanteneous feedback, and quick transition between on and off states for NO_2 gas sensing[34]. Moreover, $MoSe_2$ deposited on a flexible substrate has demonstrated selectivity for detecting NO_2 and NH_3 with high electrical properties. Gold-assisted $MoSe_2$ FETs have also been tested on human skin and connected to a flexible print circuit board for streaming and wireless recording [35].

In a study by Guo *et al.*[35], gold-assisted $MoSe_2$ field-effect transistors (FETs) were evaluated on human skin and integrated with a flexible circuit for wire-free recording and streaming.

PHOTODETECTORS:

TMDs and other 2D semiconductors like phosphorene possess excellent charge transport properties and an optical/near-infrared bandgap. Their ultra-thin monolayer thickness (<1 nm) enables them to absorb up to 10% of visible light, equivalent to 100 nm of silicon. The exfoliation and restacking of different van der Waals heterostructures offer a flexible approach to designing a new generation of optoelectronic devices. Vertically stacked p- and n-type 2D semiconductor photodiodes, including MoS_2-WSe_2 [36], MoS_2-black phosphorous [37], and MoS_2-GaTe [38], have been investigated in various configurations.

LIGHT EMITTING DEVICES:

Monolayer TMDs have limited light emission capability in one-dimensional junctions. However, vertically stacked vdWHs is able to provide longer photoactive region, making them a promising platform for photoemission and photodetection applications [32, 36, 39].

SINGLE ELECTRON TRANSISTOR:

The ideal materials for SETs are typically characterized by specific properties such as high electrical conductivity, low tunneling barrier height, and low energy relaxation time. Regarding this matter, two-dimensional semiconductors have the potential to be a favorable option for single-electron transistors (SETs) due to their layer-dependent bandgap, which provides an additional level of control. However, for metallic 2D materials like graphene, functionalization or nanoribbon structures can be employed to induce a transport gap. Till now, Graphene [40, 41], MoS_2 [42] have been used in SETs. Additionally, theoretical calculations of SETs based on 2D materials have shown potential applications in gas and hazardous chemical sensing . In these devices, the 2D material serves as a channel between the source and drain electrodes. Upon the adsorption of foreign molecules onto the channel's surface, the electrical properties of the channel, including its conductivity, can undergo significant alterations, leading to changes in the device's performance. This effect is a critical consideration in the design and operation of gas and hazardous chemical sensors, as well as other nanoelectronic devices. By leveraging the unique sensitivity of SETs to the presence of external factors, highly sensitive and selective sensors can be developed, enabling the detection of trace amounts of gas and hazardous chemicals.

1.10 IMPORTANCE OF DENSITY FUNCTIONAL THEORY (DFT)

DFT is a powerful computational package to predict and quantify physical properties of materials. By employing DFT, it is possible investigate how these physical properties may be influenced by variations in composition or external conditions. Furthermore, DFT can be utilized to optimize the structure of 2D materials to enhance their properties for targeted applications. In this manner, DFT serves as a valuable tool for advancing our understanding and utilization of 2D materials. One of the most impressive capabilities of DFT is its ability to predict the properties of materials before they have been synthesized or characterized experimentally.

In conclusion, DFT has become an essential tool in predicting, analyzing, and supporting research on two-dimensional materials. Its ability to predict the properties of materials before they have been synthesized or characterized experimentally has opened up new avenues for materials research. DFT calculations can provide valuable insight into the behavior of 2D materials and help guide experimental research towards materials with specific properties for various applications. With advancements in computational power and algorithmic development, DFT is poised to assume a progressively crucial role in the academia as well as in industry.

1.11 THESIS ORGANIZATION

The thesis is categorized into 8 chapters, in which, the Chapter 1 and 2 presents the Introduction and Methodology required for the investigation. Chapter 3 represents the detail study of synthesis process of Magnetic topological Insulator $MnBi_2Te_4$, $MnBi_4Te_7$ and $Mn_2Bi_2Te_5$ and investigation of their physical properties through magnetic and transport study, Chapter 4 shows the study of twist angle dependent electronic, magnetic, optical and transport properties of $MnBi_2Te_4/CrGeTe_3$ Van der Waals heterostructure, Chapter 5 represents the proximity induced Colossal Conductivity Modulation in Phosphorene. Chapter 6 represents the effect of various strain on Bi_2Se_3 island based nanoelectronic system, Chapter 7 represents theTemperature and frequency dependent resisitve switching property of LSMO and copper iodide nanocomposite, Chapter 8 discusses the conclusion and scope of future research of the present thesis.

2

METHODOLOGY

This chapter will discuss the experimental and theoretical techniques used during my doctoral research. The experimental techniques section will provide a comprehensive idea of the various methods used to obtain the data, including the instruments and materials used. The theoretical methodology section will cover the analytical and computational tools I used to explain the Density functional theory calculations. Overall, this chapter will offer a detailed exploration of both the experimental and theoretical methodology used in my doctoral research, providing a comprehensive understanding of the methodology and findings.

2.1 EXPERIMENTAL METHODOLOGY

The section will explain the sample preparation procedure and characterization techniques used to perform the experiments. The section is divided into three subsections;

- Subsection 2.1.1 will focus on sample preparation techniques. This subsection will cover the solid-state synthesis process, which was utilized for the synthesis of $La_{0.7}Sr_{0.3}$-MnO_3, as well as the slow cooling technique employed for the creation of single crystals of Van der Waals materials.
- Subsection 2.1.2 will focus on sample characterization techniques.
- In subsection 2.1.3, the transport and magnetic measurement setup will be discussed in detail. Additionally, there will be a brief introduction to the project aimed at integrating and automating the transport study data acquisition process via LabView. This section

will provide a panoramic overview of the electrical transport setup, the cryostat, and the vital role of LabView software in automating the entire measurement process.

2.1.1 SAMPLE SYNTHESIS TECHNIQUES

2.1.1.1 SOLID STATE SYNTHESIS

The solid-state synthesis process typically involves mixing powdered precursor materials together and heating them in a furnace to induce the desired reaction. The high temperatures and long reaction times required for solid-state synthesis are due to the slow diffusive reaction between solid reactants. However, this technique offers several benefits, including the ability to produce materials that are difficult or impossible to synthesize through other methods and providing superior control over the reaction conditions. Through solid-state synthesis we can synthesize various materials like oxides, chalcogenides, inter-metallics, etc.

Chapter 7 discusses the resistive switching behavior of the $La_{0.7}Sr_{0.3}MnO$/CuI nanocomposite. We employed solid-state synthesis to produce one of the composite system's precursors, LSMO. We procured copper iodide and the precursor chemicals (La_2O_3, $SrCO_3$, and Mn_2O_3) with a minimum purity of 99.99% from Sigma-Aldrich. To synthesize $La_{0.7}Sr_{0.3}MnO_3$ (LSMO), we first mixed stoichiometric amounts of La_2O_3, $SrCO_3$, and Mn_2O_3 thoroughly in acetone for 5 hours. Subsequently, we calcined the mixture at a temperature of 1200°C for 12 hours in a muffle furnace chamber with sufficient heating (and cooling) at approximately 3°C/min. After obtaining $La_{0.7}Sr_{0.3}MnO_3$ from the solid-state synthesis route, we further ground the calcined powder for 1 hour to achieve a homogeneous mixture.

2.1.1.2 SINGLE CRYSTAL GROWTH IN A SEALED QUARTZ TUBE

Single crystal growth is essential for developing high-quality materials. One of the techniques used to grow single crystals by sealing a quartz ampoule crucible. This process involves heating the raw materials inside a quartz ampoule that is sealed under a vacuum or inert gas. The material is heated to a high temperature, then gradually lowered to facilitate crystal growth. The quartz ampoule protects the sample from contamination and allows for a controlled cooling process. The quartz sealing method produces high-quality crystals with well-defined facets and low defect densities, making it a preferred technique for growing single crystals for research and industrial applications.

During my doctoral studies, I was assigned to construct an experimental setup for synthesizing crystals in a sealed quartz tube. The setup involved designing an assembly to hold the quartz tube in a fixed position and connect it to the turbo molecular pump using CAD software. I procured high-quality oxyacetylene and oxygen gas, ensuring they met the specifications of the quartz tube sealing process. The Mn_2Bi2Te_5, $MnBi_2Te_4$ and $MnBi_4Te_7$ crystals were grown by custom-built quartz tube sealing unit in our laboratory. The crystal growth was bagged after annealing the stoichiometric mixture of Bi_2Te_3 and α-Mn-Te in the furnace. Both $MnBi_2Te4$ and $MnBi_4Te_4$ are not thermodynamically stable at room temperature but can be achieved by quenching the meta-stable product at a temperature slightly below the melting point of the material.

A slow cooling method approach was considered for all the magnetic topological insulator-based single crystals for the characterizations and measurements purpose in the present thesis. The crystal growth mechanism completes in two steps. First, an evacuated quartz ampoule ($\approx 10^{-4}$ mbar) was considered for sealing the stoichiometric mixture of MnTe and Bi_2Te_3, which was then heated up to a high temperature. The ampoule was kept at a high temperature for two days to improve the homogeneity of the material, and then it undergoes for room-temperature quenching.

2.1.2 CHARACTERIZATION TECHNIQUES

The characterization techniques employed in this thesis include Atomic Force Microscopy (AFM), Raman Spectroscopy, X-ray Photoelectron Spectroscopy (XPS), Scanning Electron Microscopy (SEM), Transmission Electron Microscopy (TEM).

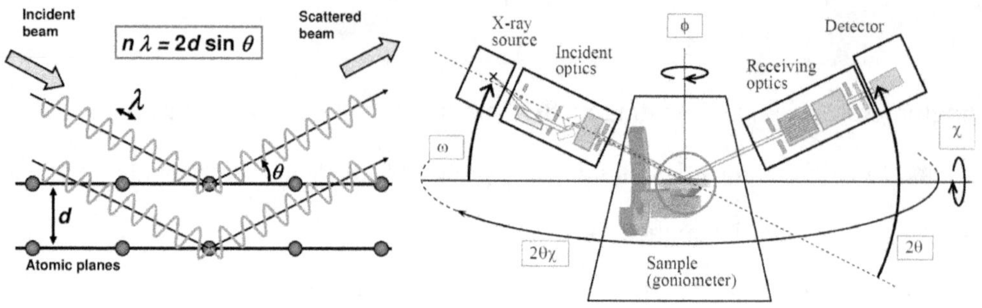

Figure 2.1: (a) Schematic representation of Bragg's equation (Adapted from [43]) (b) schematic representation of XRD diffractometer [44].

2.1.2.1 X-RAY DIFFRACTION (XRD)

XRD is a non-invasive and rapid analytical measurement used to identify phase, miller indices, atomic spacing, stress, lattice constant, and crystal structure of the crystalline specimen under investigation. The diffraction of X-rays from crystals is described by the Bragg's Law:

$$2dsin\theta = n\lambda \quad (2.1)$$

The variable 'd' represents the interplanar spacing of a set of parallel atomic planes, 'θ' (theta) is the incident angle,'n' is an integer, and 'λ' is the wavelength of the incident X-ray beam used. Copper is the most frequent target material for single-crystal diffraction, with Cu K-α radiation = 1.54 used in XRD. An X-ray diffractometer consists of three components: X-ray source, specimen, and detector, all located on the circumference of an imaginary circle called the focusing circle. The angle between the plane of the specimen and the incident X-ray is θ, while the angle between the incident X-ray source and the detector is 2θ. The radius of the focusing circle is not constant but depends on the 2θ value (see Figure.2.1.(a)). The diffractometer circle is another imaginary circle defined such that the specimen is at the center, with the source and detector on the circumference, and its radius is constant.

2.1.2.2 ATOMIC FORCE MICROSCOPY

AFM is a technique used to study surface properties of a sample, such as thickness and roughness, by measuring atomic interactions between the sample and a cantilever tip. The

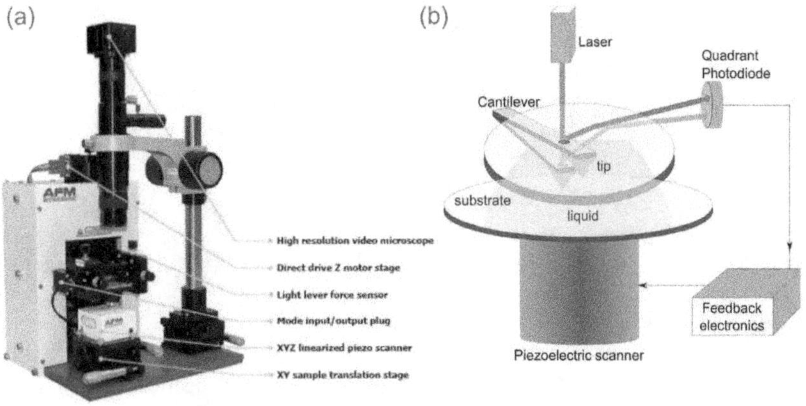

Figure 2.2: (a) Schematic of atomic force microscope. (b) Working principle of AFM

cantilever tip is scanned across the sample surface and its deflection is monitored using a laser and quadrant photodiode. The resulting height profile of the sample surface can be used to produce AFM topography. AFM has a high resolution, suitable for characterizing 2D materials, and works in three modes: contact, tapping, and non-contact. In this thesis, AFM was used to determine the layer thickness of MBT layers in Chapter 6 using a NanoScope-6 MultiMode 8-HR in tapping mode with Nanosensors PointProbe® Plus tapping Mode probes.

2.1.2.3 X-RAY PHOTOELECTRON SPECTROSCOPY (XPS)

X-ray photoelectron spectroscopy (XPS) is a surface characterization technique that determines the elemental compositions, chemical valence states, and element ratios within a material by irradiating it with X-rays and measuring the kinetic energy and number of emitted electrons (Figure.2.3.(a)). The X-ray beam's limited wavelength range (0.01-10 nm) restricts the measurement depth to 0-10 nm. XPS is suitable for investigating 2D material surfaces, which are usually less than 10 nm thick. XPS is costly because it requires high or ultra-high vacuum conditions.

2.1.2.4 SCANNING ELECTRON MICROSCOPY (SEM)

SEM uses a beam of electrons to create high-resolution images of the surface of a sample. The new generation SEM is called FESEM, which has higher resolution and energy range. It uses a field emission gun as an electron source. It can also work in a low potential difference

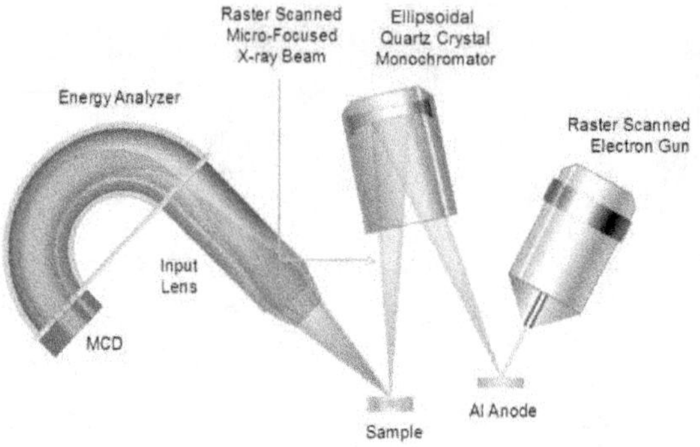

Figure 2.3: (a) Schematic of X-ray photoelectron spectroscopy.

in the order of 0.02-5 kV, which helps to reduce the charging effect in a conductive sample and save it from possible destruction by an electron beam. Simultaneously, they give high resolution with the help of an in-lens detector. FESEM is a versatile instrument that uses a beam of electrons to scan samples in a parallel pattern and investigate their microstructure, morphology, and chemical composition. FESEM uses high energy beam ($\approx$ 20 KeV) electrons produced by an electron gun and are to be incident on a solid surface and generate signals at the specimen surface. When electron beams strike the specimen, multiple interactions occur, ejecting electrons and photons from the sample. These collected/emitted electrons create the image on a Cathode Ray Tube (CRT). These signals have information about the specimen's surface topography, elemental composition, high-resolution images, and electrical behavior on a specimen surface. The type of signals generated by FESEM includes secondary electrons, Auger electrons, characteristic X-rays, and back-scattered electrons (BSEs).

The field emission gun is used as an electron source. It can also work in a low potential difference in the order of 0.02-5 kV, which helps to reduce the charging effect in a conductive sample and save it from possible destruction by an electron beam. Simultaneously, they give high resolution with the help of an in-lens detector, as shown in Figure. 2.4. The grain size (t) of the given sample is given by,

$$t = \frac{1.56 \times L}{M \times N} \tag{2.2}$$

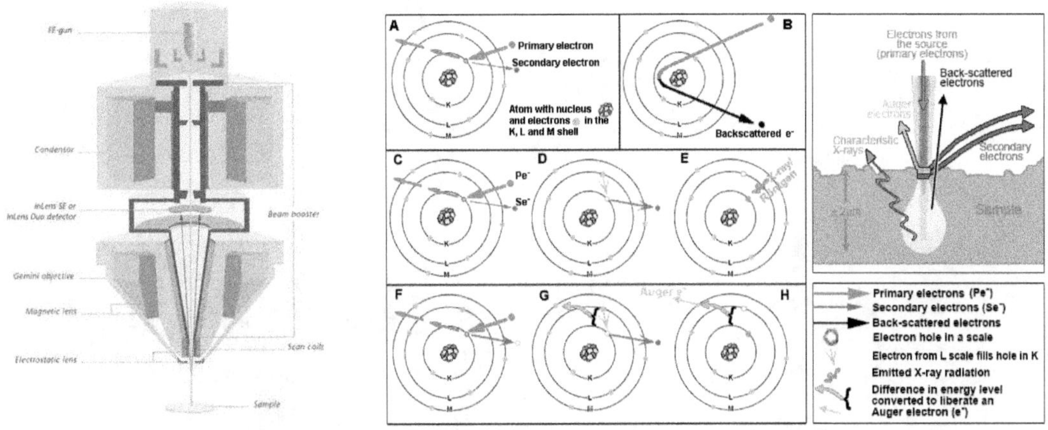

Figure 2.4: (a) Schematic cross-section of Gemini optical column with beam booster, In-lens detector and Gemini objective (Adapted from [45]). (b) The electron-specimen interaction volume. The interactions between the electron and sample are shown on the right (Adapted from [46])

Where L is the length of a line, M is the magnification and N is the number of grain boundaries touching the line. SEM provides information on the topography, morphology, composition, and crystallographic information of a sample. This includes details on the surface texture and features, particle size and shape, element composition, and atom arrangement in the material. See Figure 2.4 for an example image.

2.1.2.5 ENERGY DISPERSIVE X-RAY ANALYSIS (EDX) METHOD

EDX is used with SEM to determine the elemental composition of materials by analyzing the X-rays emitted when the electron beam interacts with a sample. While it is not an accurate quantitative technique, it can indicate the presence of elements within a sample.

In this thesis, EDX analysis was conducted with the help of the JEOL JSM-6500F field emission SEM operated at 15 kV using an EDAX detector and EDAX Genesis software for the elemental assignment of signals. In chapter 3, the concentration of LSMO/CuI composite, and in Chapter 4, the elemental composition and layered structure have been assessed by EDX.

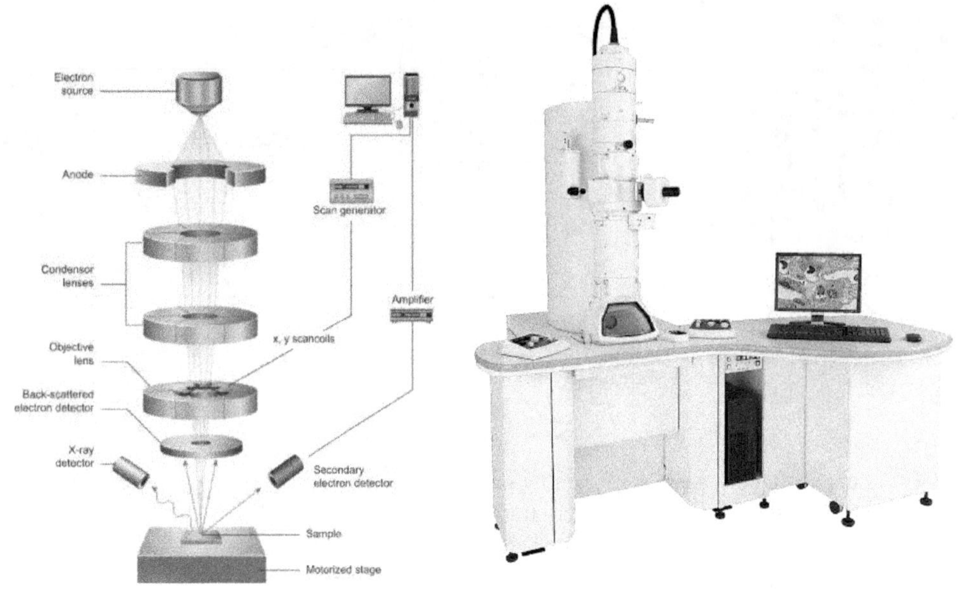

Figure 2.5: The JEOL JEM-1400 series 120kV Transmission Electron Microscope

2.1.2.6 HIGH-RESOLUTION TRANSMISSION ELECTRON MICROSCOPE (HRTEM)

TEM is a powerful technique for material characterization that utilizes high energy electrons to investigate the internal structure and crystallinity of thin specimens based on the principle of electron diffraction. The electron beam is focused by the condenser lens and restricted by the aperture to eliminate high-angle electrons. The objective lens generates a diffraction pattern at the back focal plane that is magnified and displayed on a phosphor screen through Fourier transform. SAED is a complimentary technique that determines lattice parameters. The JEOL-2010 ultra-high-resolution transmission electron microscope operates at 200kV, has a lattice resolution of 0.14nm, and a point-to-point resolution of 0.12nm. It has multiple modes including Bright-Field, Dark-Field, High resolution, SAED, and CBED modes, with a resolution of $1.5x10^6$. Nitrogen is used for anti-contamination to protect the filament from volatile samples.

Figure 2.6: (a) Micromanipulated probe station, (b) Interior of the probe station and (c) Liquid Nitrogen transfer system.

2.1.3 MAGNETIC AND TRANSPORT MEASUREMENT

2.1.3.1 MICROMANIPULATED PROBE STATION

The Janis micro-manipulated probe station model ST-500 has been used to perform the transport study. The system contained a vacuum chamber with four entry probe arms and a clear-view window on top of the chamber. The continuous flow ST-500 cryostat includes a cold head with a sample mount and a thermal radiation shield surrounding the sample mounting area. The sample mounting stage holds a silicon diode temperature sensor supplied with a Lakeshore 336 temperature controller for controlling the temperature of the sample mount. A high-efficiency liquid nitrogen transfer line is supplied with the system (see Figure. 2.6).

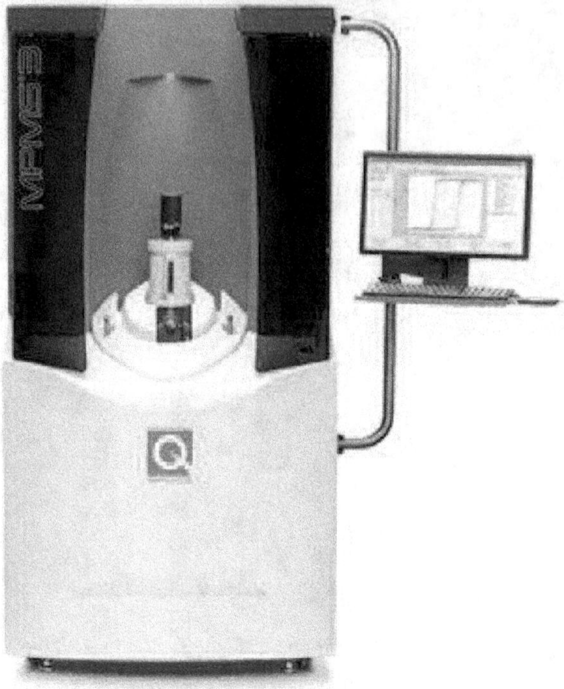

Figure 2.7: MPMS SQUID VSM dc Magnetometer

2.1.3.2 MPMS SQUID VSM DC MAGNETOMETER

The squid VSM dc magnetometer is a scientific instrument used to measure the magnetic properties of materials.

The MPMS SQUID VSM magnetometer has $\leq 10^{-8}$ emu sensitivity and 4 second data averaging. It combines the speed of a Vibrating Sample Magnetometer with the sensitivity of a SQUID magnetometer, and offers advances in data acquisition, temperature control and magnetic field control. The system can be cooled with a standard liquid helium cooling system or a 4He-based Pulse Tube cooler. The FastLab™ data acquisition, RapidTemp™ temperature control and QuickSwitch™ magnet control allow for quick and accurate measurements.

2.1.3.3 4K CRYOSTAT

In our lab we used ColdEdge cryostate with RDK-101D cold head. It is a two-stage Gifford-McMahon cycle cryo-refrigerator. The page first stage cold station has a refrigeration capacity

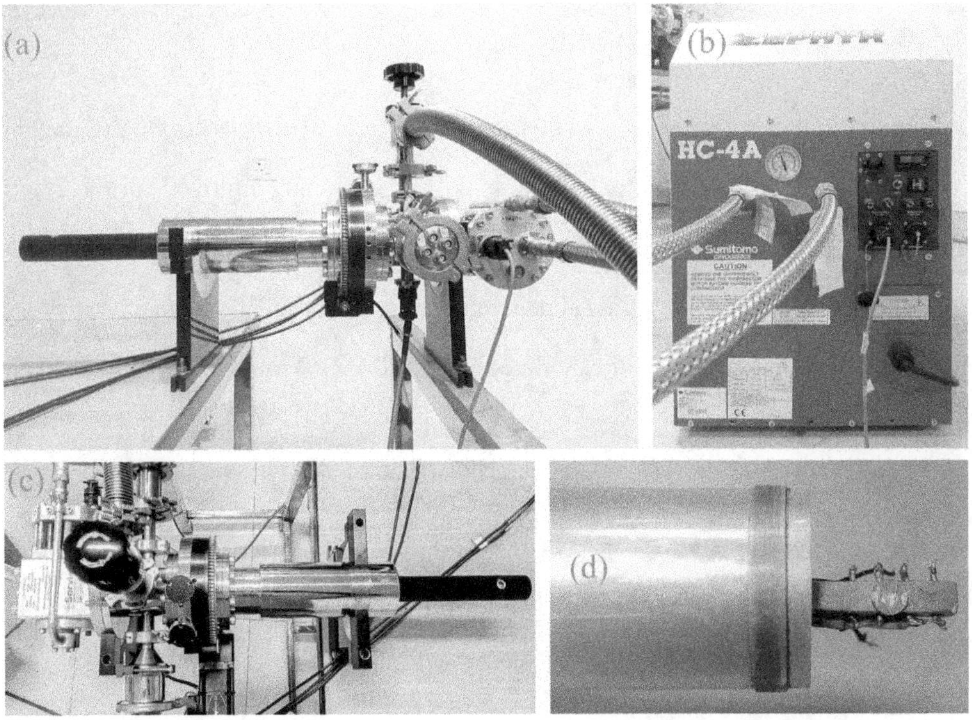

Figure 2.8: a) Image of 4K crystat , (b) Image of helium compresor, (c) top view of the cryostat and (d) Image of sample stage with a sample attached to the sample stage with Aapiezon grease.

of 60 K, while the second stage can reach 4.2 K. RDK-101D three main modules: the drive unit, cylinder, and displacer-regenerator assembly, which is inside the cylinder. Helium gas compressed under high pressure is supplied from the compressor unit to the cold head via a gas supply connector, then passed to the displacer-regenerator assembly motor housing, pushed to the crankcase, and returned to the compressor unit through the return connector.

We have used 4K cryostat for resitance, differential conductance vs voltage and Current vs Voltage measurement and integrated Lakeshore 336 temperature controller through Labview.

2.2 THEORETICAL METHODOLOGY

This section will outline the theoretical methodology. Here, a brief description of the application of the DFT for atomic scale calculations will be given as employed for the electronic structure calculations in this thesis. We will then describe electron transport with quantum transport theory based on non-equilibrium Green's function (NEGF). The magnetic properties of the 2D magnetic materials were calculated by employing Monte Carlo simulation based on the 2D Ising model.

2.2.1 DENSITY FUNCTIONAL THEORY (DFT)

DFT has made its way to the central stage in quantum chemistry and condensed matter physics. The main reason behind this is the accuracy and computational economy of the calculations, which make the choice of DFT natural and practical. In this chapter, we elucidate the theoretical background of the DFT and the computational method, which has been employed during the electronic structure and transport calculations in the thesis. In the first part of this chapter, an overview of the main theorems behind the DFT is presented. Further, a brief description of the application of the DFT for atomic scale calculations is given, as employed for the electronic structure calculations in this thesis. The chapter ends with a glimpse of theory, describing electron transport with quantum transport theory based on non-equilibrium Green's function (NEGF). The magnetic properties of the 2D magnetic materials, Van der Waals heterostructure, by employing Monte Carlo simulation based on 2D ising model.

2.2.2 INTRODUCTION

In order to determine a material system's electronic properties, the well-known Schrödinger equation

$$\hat{H}\psi(r_1, r_2, \ldots.., R_1, R_1, \ldots) = E\psi(r_1, r_2, \ldots.., R_1, R_1, \ldots) \tag{2.3}$$

Where Ψ(r, R) is the wavefunction of an interacting pair of electrons at position r and position R of the nucleus. For many-body system, the Hamiltonian can be expressed as:

$$\hat{H} = \underbrace{-\sum_{j=1}^{N} \frac{\hbar^2}{2M_j} \nabla^2_{R_j}}_{\hat{T}_n} \underbrace{- \sum_{i=1}^{n} \frac{\hbar^2}{2m_i} \nabla^2_{r_i}}_{\hat{T}_e}$$

$$\underbrace{\underbrace{+\frac{1}{2}\sum_{j=1}^{n}\sum_{j\neq j'}^{n} \frac{Z_j Z'_j e^2}{|R_j - R'_j|}}_{\hat{V}_{nn}} \underbrace{+\frac{1}{2}\sum_{i=1}^{n}\sum_{i\neq i'}^{n} \frac{e^2}{|r_i - r'_i|}}_{\hat{V}_{ee}} \underbrace{-\sum_{j=1}^{N}\sum_{i=1}^{n} \frac{Z_j e^2}{|R_j - r_i|}}_{\hat{V}_{en}}}_{\hat{V}} \tag{2.4}$$

Where r_i and R_j signify the position vector of ith electron and j^{th} nucleus of a system of N atoms with n electrons. M_j, m_i, Z and *e* represents the mass of the nucleus, the mass of the electron, the atomic number and the charge of the electrons, respectively. The kinetic energy of the nuclei and energy of the electron is denoted by the first and second in the equation.2.4. The second term denotes the electron's energy, the third term denotes the Coulomb interaction's energy term between nuclei, the fourth term denotes the Coulomb interaction's energy term between electrons, and the fifth term denotes the Coulomb interaction's energy term between nuclei and electrons.

The Born-Oppenheimer approximation simplified the many-body Hamiltonian comprising both ions and electrons to a many-body Hamiltonian comprising electrons only. However, the solution of the resulting electronic Hamiltonian given in Equation 2.4 remains challenging, as it requires solving second-order differential equations for N electrons. Hence, it becomes necessary to explore alternative methods for solving the many-body problem by constraining the number of degrees of freedom.

2.2.3 FOUNDATION TO DENSITY FUNCTIONAL THEORY (DFT)

Hohenberg and Kohn's groundbreaking publication marked the genesis of the contemporary Density Functional Theory (DFT). This theory aims to supplant the intricate and arduous wavefunction of many electrons, containing 3N variables (where N represents the number of electrons and each electron has three spatial variables), with the more manageable and straightforward functional of electron density, having only three variables. The introduction of this new system drastically reduces the number of variables to be managed to a mere three, which is significantly more manageable than the prodigious 3N variables.

2.2.3.1 HOHENBERG–KOHN THEOREM

In the first theorem, Hohenberg and Kohn suggested that ground state energy is uniquely related to electron density, i.e., a function of electron density. Their second theorem demonstrated that ground state energy might be attained by minimizing the system's energy in accordance with the electron density.

Theorem I: The ground state particle density $n(r)$ uniquely determines the external potential $V_{ext}(r)$ for interacting particles in an external potential, except for a constant. This theorem establishes a direct correspondence between the ground state wave function and electron density of a many-particle system.

$$n(\mathbf{r}) = N \int d^3r_1 d^3r_2 ....d^3r_N \psi(r_1, r_2....r_N)\psi^*(r_1, r_2....r_N) \tag{2.5}$$

Theorem II: A universal energy function $E[n(r)]$ can be constructed for the density $n(r)$, effective for $V_{ext}(r)$. The exact ground state energy of the system for a given $V_{ext}(r)$ is the global minimum value of this function. The density $n(r)$ that minimizes the energy functional corresponds to the exact ground state density $n_0(r)$, thereby minimizing the electronic energy of the system.

$$E = E[n_0(\mathbf{r})] = min[E[n_0(\mathbf{r})]] \tag{2.6}$$

$$E = \frac{\delta E[n(\mathbf{r})]}{\delta n(\mathbf{r})} \tag{2.7}$$

This indicates that the ground state electron density minimizes the system's total electronic energy.

2.2.3.2 KOHN–SHAM EQUATIONS

Kohn and Sham further simplified the problem of multi-electron systems by transforming it into an equivalent non-interacting electron system in an effective potential. This potential comprises of the external potential along with the contributions from the electron-electron Coulomb interactions, including the exchange and correlation interactions. The total energy function is given by:

$$E[n(\mathbf{r})] = T_{IN}[n(r)] + E_{HF}[n(\mathbf{r})] + E_{ext}[n(\mathbf{r})] + E_{XC}[n(\mathbf{r})] \quad (2.8)$$

The functional comprises four terms. The first term explicitly depends on density and represents the kinetic energy of non-interacting electrons. The second and third terms are the Hartree-Fock contribution, which describes the interaction among the remaining electrons. The last term, known as the exchange and correlation functional, takes into account all many-body effects. Although its analytical expression is unknown, the Kohn-Sham formalism splits the implicit terms into the kinetic and Coulomb energy of independent electrons, along with an additional term that accounts for the difference:

$$H_{KS} = \frac{\hbar^2}{2m_i}\nabla^2 + \frac{e^2}{4\pi\epsilon_o}\int \frac{n(\mathbf{r})}{|r - r_0|}d\mathbf{r} + V_{ext}[n(\mathbf{r})] + V_{XC}[n(\mathbf{r})] \quad (2.9)$$

$E_{xc}[n(r)]$, comprises everything else which is named exchange and correlation energy:

$$V_{XC}[n(\mathbf{r})] = \frac{\delta E_{XC}[n(\mathbf{r})]}{\delta n(\mathbf{r})} \quad (2.10)$$

Solving the KS equations self-consistently via iteration allows us to calculate the ground state energy of a system using the electron density if we know the exchange and correlation energy, $E_{xc}[n(r)]$. This method ensures that lowest ground state density will be obtained.

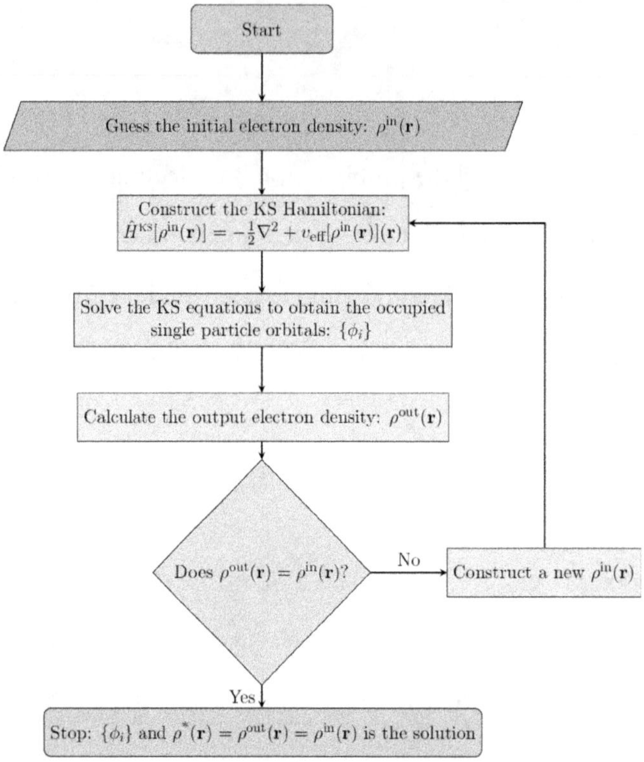

Figure 2.9: Flow chart for nth iteration in the self-consistent process.

2.2.3.3 SELF-CONSISTENT FIELD METHOD

First, the effective potential needs to be known to solve a Kohn- Sham equation, which depends on electron density. To estimate the electron density, single-electron wave functions must be computed from Kohn–Sham equation. Thus it becomes a loop of equations, which can be solved by an iterative method until a convergence in the electron density is achieved. By meeting a ground state energy convergence condition, we can confirm the convergence in the electron density. This iteration process is known as a self-consistent field (SCF) cycle.

2.2.4 EXCHANGE-CORRELATION FUNCTIONALS

To solve Kohn–Sham equations, the exchange-correlation energy E_{xc} includes for the remaining electronic energy not taken into consideration in non-interacting kinetic and electrostatic terms. E_{xc} can be written as:

$$E_{XC} = E_X + E_C \tag{2.11}$$

The exchange-correlation energy, resulting from the sum of two kinds of energies, is crucial in determining the accuracy of DFT computations. Approximations for this energy include the local density approximation (LDA) and the generalized gradient approximation (GGA). Four spin versions of each function exist: non-polarized, spin-polarized, noncollinear, and noncollinear with spin-orbit coupling.

2.2.4.1 LOCAL DENSITY APPROXIMATIONS (LDA)

As the exact form of E_{xc} is unknown, approximations is required. Kohn and Sham introduced a formalism known as LDA [47] in which they suggested that the exchange-correlation energy density could be treated as a homogeneous electron gas and described by a locally homogeneous expression. They approximated the electron density at each point in space is the same as that of a uniform electron gas with the same density. It is described as

$$E_{xc}^{LDA} = \int n(r)\epsilon_{xc}^{hom}[n(r)]dr, \tag{2.12}$$

ϵ_{xc} is exchange-correlation energy density at a local position r is approximated as the energy density of a homogeneous electron gas with the same locally determined density, denoted as ϵ_{xc}^{hom}. The ϵ_{xc}^{hom} is decomposed into exchange (ϵ_x) and correlation (ϵ_c) terms, with the exchange part computable analytically but the correlation part still unknown. Therefore, the numerical form of ϵ_{xc} is obtained through Monte-Carlo calculations and interpolation schemes.

2.2.4.2 GENERALIZED GRADIENT APPROXIMATIONS (GGA)

Hohenberg and Kohn [48] proposed augmenting the LDA by incorporating the local density gradient into the exchange and correlation expression, which forms the basis of GGA [49, 50]. In GGA, the exchange-correlation density is a function of not only the electronic density

$n(r)$ but also the gradient of the electronic density $\nabla n(r)$. The GGA exchange-correlation energy is obtained by modifying the LDA energy density and can be represented as:

$$E_{xc}^{GGA} = \int n(r)\epsilon_{xc}^{GGA}[n(r)dr, \nabla n(r)]drE_{xc}^{GGA} = \int \epsilon_{xc}^{hom} F_{xc}[n(r)dr, \nabla n(r)]n(r)]dr \tag{2.13}$$

2.2.4.3 COULOMB CORRECTED LDA/(GGA)+U APPROXIMATION

LDA and GGA fail to predict electronic properties of strongly correlated systems, like transition and rear earth metal, due to their inability to handle partial d or f orbitals. To address this, orbital-dependent potentials for d and f electrons should be used to represent strongly correlated systems accurately. The electrons in the LDA (GGA)+U technique are grouped into two types: orbital-dependent localized d and f electrons, which should be utilized to explain the $d-d$ or $f-f$ interaction, and delocalized s, p electrons, which are predicted using the LDA/GGA method. The Hubbard on-site interaction U is computed for the d or f orbital by differentiating the LDA/GGA eigenvalues with respect to the occupation numbers. Then, we include an additional term to the exchange-correlation functional:

$$E_{\mathrm{U}} = \frac{1}{2}\sum U_{\mu}(n_{\mu} - n_{\mu}^{2}) \tag{2.14}$$

where, n_{μ} is atomic shell projection, U_{μ} Hubbard U parameter U_{μ}, E_U is the energy term that is zero for fully occupied or unoccupied shells and positive for fractionally populated shells. When energy levels move away from the Fermi Level or the state broadening reduces, electrons become more localized, leading to a decrease in energy if the states become entirely occupied or vacant. Empirically, the value of U can be adjusted to match experimental data.

2.2.4.4 META-GGA FUNCTIONAL

Kohn-Sham energy eigenvalues derived from GGA is notorious for severely underestimating band gaps. On the other hand, recent developments in meta-GGA functionals have enabled us to compute exact band gaps. The meta-GGA (MGGA) functional family improves the accuracy of the GGA approximation by meta-GGA (MGGA) family of functionals by adding one or both of the Laplacian of the density ($\nabla^2 n(r)$) and kinetic energy density ($\frac{1}{2}\sum f_\alpha |\nabla \psi_\alpha(r)|^2$)

In chapter 6, we utilized strongly-constrained and appropriately-normed (SCAN), a Meta-GGA functional to compute the electronic characteristics of the MBT/CGT heterostructure. The SCAN meta-GGA functional is a significant development since it is the only semilocal exchange-correlation functional that meets 17 known exact restrictions for being a semilocal functional. Furthermore, SCAN is 'appropriately normed,' capturing interactions in rare-gas atoms and non-bonded systems.

SCAN meta-GGA has been proven to be smart enough to simulate a wide range of physical structures without being suited to any bonded system in calculations of energetics for diversely bound systems. The benefits of this meta-GGA technique include that calculations using a meta-GGA are substantially less computationally intensive than hybrid functional calculations for materials, and the kinetic-energy density can offer information regarding orbital characteristics.

2.2.5 PSEUDOPOTENTIALS AND BASIS SET

In materials, valence electrons mostly affect physical properties, despite core electrons being present. Pseudopotentials replace the strong Coulomb potential of the nucleus and tightly bound core electrons with a softer effective ionic potential, which only affects valence electrons. This is done through the screening effect of the core electrons. The Schrödinger equation used in pseudopotential method is

$$\hat{V}^{ps} = \hat{V}_{eff} + \sum_{c}(E_v - E_c)|\psi_c >< \psi_v| = V_{eff} + \hat{V}_{nl} \tag{2.15}$$

$\hat{V}^{ps}$ and $\hat{V}_{nl}$ represents the true potentiallocalized repulsive potential in the core region. So it negates the strong attractive nuclear Coulomb potential and softens the core potential, resulting in a weaker pseudopotential and nodeless pseudo wavefunction.

Bloch's theorem allows the expansion of electronic wavefunctions using a discrete plane-wave basis set at each k-point. KS-DFT replaces the true wave function with a non-interacting model, represented by a single Slater determinant, resulting in the same ground state energy. However, the wave function takes on different shapes in the core and valence regions, making it crucial to select a basis set that accurately reflects its features (see Figure. 2.10). Now, we will briefly discuss about different basis sets.

2.2.5.1 PLANE WAVE BASIS SET

In KS-DFT formalism, the wave function ψ of an electron moving in a effective potential of a periodic lattice can be expressed as a sum of plane waves:

$$\psi_k(r) = e^{ikr} u_{ik}(r), where \tag{2.16}$$

$$u_{ik}(r) = \sum_G c_i G^{iG.r} \tag{2.17}$$

The PW basis set allows expressing the periodic function $u_{ik}(r)$ as a sum of plane waves with the same periodicity. Thus, the KS orbitals can be represented as a linear combination of plane waves,

$$\psi_{ik}(r) = \sum_G c_{ik}(G) \times \frac{1}{\sqrt{\Omega}} e^{i(K+G).r} \tag{2.18}$$

where c_{ik} is where the expansion coefficients $c_{ik}(G)$ are multiplied by the normalized plane wave $e^{i(K+G).r}$ with reciprocal lattice vector G. The normalization factor $\frac{1}{\sqrt{\Omega}}$ accounts for the periodic boundary condition in a large volume Ω, which can be infinite. The Bloch wave vector k is also involved in the expression.

2.2.5.2 PROJECTOR AUGMENTED WAVE BASIS SET

The PAW technique simplifies the calculation of all-electron properties by transforming the rapid oscillations of valence wavefunctions around ion cores into smooth wavefunctions, making them more computationally convenient. This is done while retaining the flexibility of

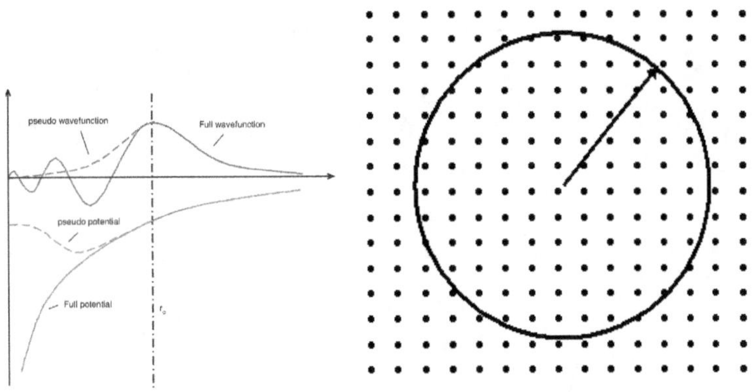

Figure 2.10: (a) Schematic of the idea of pseudopotential. At the cut-off radius r_c and beyond, the pseudo wave function corresponds with the real or full valence wave function. (b) Schematic representation of the cutoff energy concept.

the augmented wave method, resulting in a simpler energy and potential independent base. The approach is analogous to switching from the Schrödinger to the Heisenberg picture.

2.2.5.3 LINEAR COMBINATION OF ATMIC ORBITALS (LCAO) BASIS SET

Plane-wave methods are computationally demanding due to the requirement of a larger number of plane waves and their extension throughout space, making them unsuitable for large systems. An alternative approach is offered by real space basis sets, which have a more natural physical appearance. In particular, for solid-state physics calculations involving periodic and translationally invariant systems, the LCAO expansion can be carried out in real space using the Bloch theorem. The LCAO basis set can be expressed as a suitable alternative. The LCAO basis set can be written as:

$$\phi_{nlm}(r) = R_{nl} Y_{lm}(r), \tag{2.19}$$

The LCAO basis set can be improved by adjusting the size and shape of the basis or by incorporating higher angular momentum polarization functions. The inclusion of polarization functions compensates for deformations resulting from bond formation in molecules and solids, leading to more precise calculations. The polarization function has higher angular momentum than occupied orbitals. It polarizes orbitals one unit lower, such as p-orbitals for s-orbitals and d-orbitals for p-orbitals.

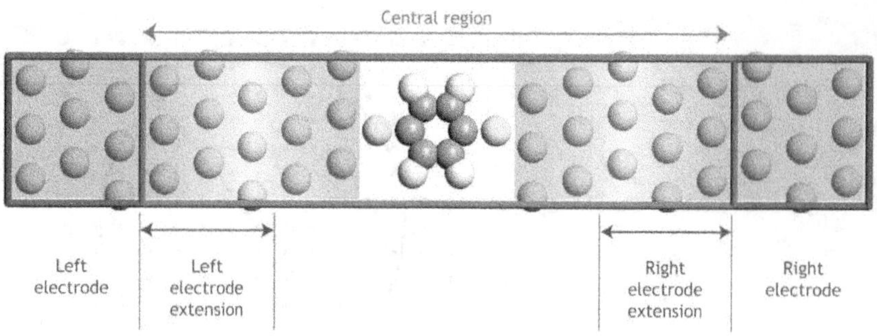

Figure 2.11: Two-probe device with periodic system in transport direction. Central region has left and right electrode extensions with periodic atom positions

2.3 QUANTUM TRANSPORT THEORY

The transport of electrons in nanoelectronic devices involves both classical and quantum mechanical behavior. One of the key concepts in this theory is the division of the material into three distinct regions: the ballistic region, the elastic and coherent region, and the inelastic and incoherent region. In the ballistic region, particles move freely without experiencing any scattering, allowing for coherent transport. In the elastic and coherent region, particles still do not undergo any significant scattering, but they may experience some degree of reflection or refraction at material interfaces. In the inelastic and incoherent region, particles experience significant scattering, resulting in energy loss and a breakdown of coherence. Understanding the behavior of particles in each of these regions is crucial for developing new materials and technologies, such as quantum computers and advanced electronic devices.

2.3.1 LANDAUER-BUTTIKER FORMULA

The Landauer-B*ü*ttiker formula [51, 52] is a fundamental result in quantum transport theory that relates the conductance of a device to its electronic properties. It states that the conductance of a device is proportional to the number of electronic modes available for transport through the device, and inversely proportional to the resistance of each mode. The Landauer-Buttiker formula is based on the concept of transmission probability, which describes the likelihood that an electron passing through the device will be transmitted from one side to the other. The formula takes into account both the ballistic and diffusive transport regimes, and can be applied to a wide range of devices, including those with complex geometries and interactions between electrons. According to Landauer-Büttiker formula the current can be calculated as:

$$I = \frac{2e}{\hbar} \int_{-eV/2}^{eV/2} T(E,V)[f_L(E-\mu_L) - f_R(E-\mu_R)]dE \tag{2.20}$$

T(E,V) is the transmission function at energy E and bias voltage V, $f_{L/R}(E,\mu_{L/R})$ represents the Fermi distribution, μ_L and μ_R are the electrochemical potentials of the left and right electrodes, respectively. The electrical conductance can be expressed as:

$$G = I/V = \frac{2e^2}{h} \int T(\epsilon) \frac{-\partial f(\epsilon)}{\partial(\epsilon)} d\epsilon \tag{2.21}$$

2.3.2 NON-EQUILIBRIUM GREEN'S FUNCTION (NEGF) METHOD

NEGF is a theoretical framework utilized to explain the transport of electrons across a system, regardless of whether the system is in thermal equilibrium or not. NEGF is based on the density matrix formalism and uses Green's function to describe the response of a system to an external perturbation. It allows for the calculation of electron transport properties, such as conductance, current, and noise, under non-equilibrium conditions that is crucial for the development of novel spintronics and optoelectronic devices.

The equation for the lesser Green's function is given by:

$$G^<(t_1,t_2) = \frac{i}{\hbar} \int_{-\infty}^{\infty} d\varepsilon, e^{\frac{i}{\hbar}\varepsilon(t_1-t_2)} \Sigma_L(\varepsilon) G^r(\varepsilon,t_1,t_2) \Sigma_R(\varepsilon) f(\varepsilon-\mu_L) +$$

$$\frac{i}{\hbar} \int_{-\infty}^{\infty} d\varepsilon, e^{\frac{i}{\hbar}\varepsilon(t_1-t_2)} \Sigma_L(\varepsilon) G^a(\varepsilon,t_1,t_2) \Sigma_R(\varepsilon)[1 - f(\varepsilon-\mu_L)]$$

where $G^<$ is the lesser Green's function, G^r is the retarded Green's function, G^a is the advanced Green's function, Σ_L and Σ_R are the self-energies of the left and right electrodes, respectively, f is the Fermi-Dirac distribution function, and μ_L is the chemical potential of the left electrode.

$$\begin{pmatrix} G^r & G^< \\ 0 & G^a \end{pmatrix} = \begin{pmatrix} E - H_0 - \Sigma^r & -\Sigma^< \\ 0 & E - H_0 - \Sigma^a \end{pmatrix} \tag{2.22}$$

E is the energy of the electrons, H_0 is the Hamiltonian of the isolated system, and Σ^r, $\Sigma^<$, and Σ^a is the self-energies, which describe the interactions of the system with its environment.

The retarded Green's function describes the propagation of an electron from an initial state to a final state through the system, while the advanced Green's function describes the propagation of an electron from a final state to an initial state. The lesser Green's function describes the probability that an electron enters the system in a certain state and leaves in another state.

The current through the device is then given by:

$$I = \frac{2e}{h}\int_{-\infty}^{\infty} d\varepsilon, \mathrm{Tr}[\Gamma_L(\varepsilon)G^<(t,t)] - \mathrm{Tr}[\Gamma_R(\varepsilon)G^<(t,t)]$$

where I is the current, e is the electron charge, h is Planck's constant, Γ_L and Γ_R are the broadening functions of the left and right electrodes, respectively, and Tr denotes the trace of the matrix.

2.4 SOFTWARE AND PACKAGES

In this thesis, we have used sevral software such as Quantum espresso, Quantum-Atomistix Tool Kit, VASP, and coding language like python to plot and evaluate the electronic, transport of 2D-material and its van der Waals heterostructure.

3

STRUCTURAL, MAGNETIC, AND TRANSPORT STUDY OF ANTIFERROMAGNETIC TOPOLOGICAL INSULATOR $MNBI_2TE_4$, $MNBI_4TE_7$, AND $MN_2BI_2TE_5$

3.1 INTRODUCTION

The intersection of magnetism and topology has the potential to give rise to intricate magnetic configurations like vortices, Weyl semimetals, and skyrmions, in both real and reciprocal momentum spaces. The interplay between topology and magnetism in MTIs offers a unique opportunity to observe exotic phenomena like quantized anomalous Hall effect, axion insulator, and Majorana modes, when time-reversal symmetry breaks down below the magnetic critical temperature. Despite the potential for magnetism to break time-reversal symmetry, certain magnetic orderings can preserve "equivalent" time-reversal symmetry, further restricting bulk bands and safeguarding the Z_2 topological properties of MTIs. The interplay between magnetism and topology is discussed extensively in subsection.1.7.6 of Chapter 1.

The objective of this chapter is to study the synthesis, structural characterization, transport, and magnetic properties of three magnetic topological insulators (MTIs): $MnBi_2Te_4$, $MnBi_4Te_7$, and $Mn_2Bi_2Te_5$. Before delving into the "Results and Discussion" section, we briefly review some experimental findings regarding these materials.

$MnBi_2Te_4$: $MnBi_2Te_4$ is a layered material consisting of Mn and Bi atoms arranged in a honeycomb lattice with lattice parameters a = b = 4.314 Å and c = 40.741 Å, belonging to the space group of $R\bar{3}m$ (No. 166) [53]. Each layer comprises of a block of septuple

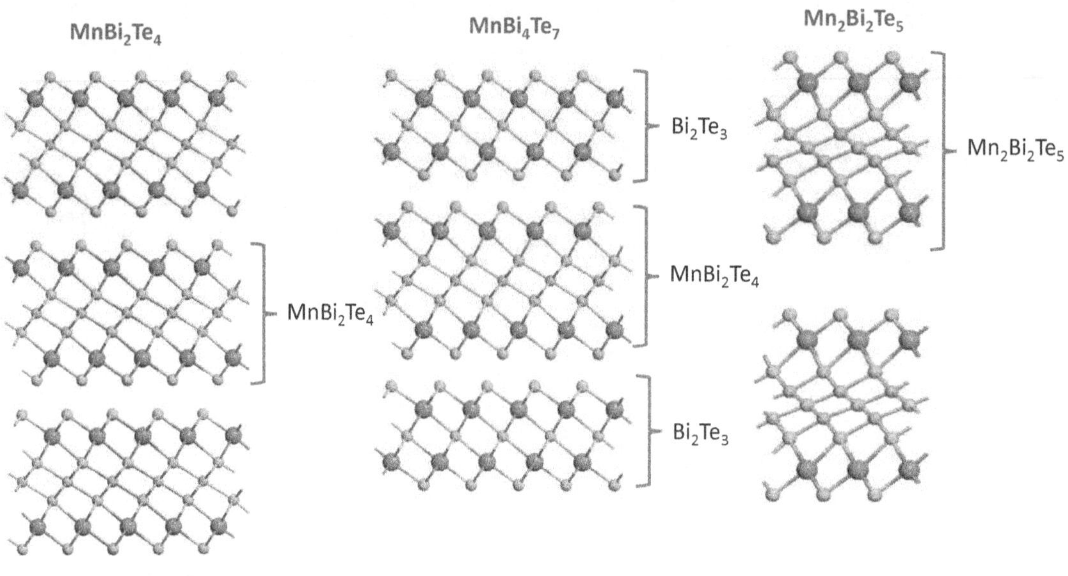

Figure 3.1: Crystal structure of (a) $MnBi_2Te_4$, (b) $MnBi_4Te_7$, and (c) $Mn_2Bi_2Te_5$

layer (see Figure. 3.1) where each layer is ferromagnetic and coupled with neighboring layer antiferromagnetically. The magnetism arises because of the Mn atoms with a $3d^5$ electronic configuration.

$MnBi_4Te_7$: $MnBi_4Te_7$ has a tetragonal crystal structure (space group is $P\bar{3}m1$, no. 164; a = b = 4.3453 Å, c = 23.705 Å) [54]. $MnBi_4Te_7$ is also a layered material that consists of alternating layer of $MnBi_2Te_4$ and Bi_2Te_3 arranged in a 1:1 ratio (see Figure. 3.1). $MnBi_4Te_7$ exhibited antiferromagnetic nature below 13K.

$Mn_2Bi_2Te_5$: $Mn_2Bi_2Te_5$ exhibits a rhombohedral crystal structure that is layered in nature, characterized by a space group of $p\bar{3}m1$ (no. 164) and lattice parameters a = b = 4.288 Å and c = 17.150 Å. This material displays antiferromagnetic behavior with a Néel temperature of 24 K. The magnetic properties of $Mn_2Bi_2Te_5$ originate from the presence of Mn atoms, which possess a $3d^5$ electronic configuration.

3.2 EXPERIMENTAL SECTION

3.2.1 SYNTHESIS PROCEDURE

Solid-state approaches for synthesizing ternary intermetallic compounds face the challenge of achieving even element distribution. To overcome this, we grew high-quality single crystals of

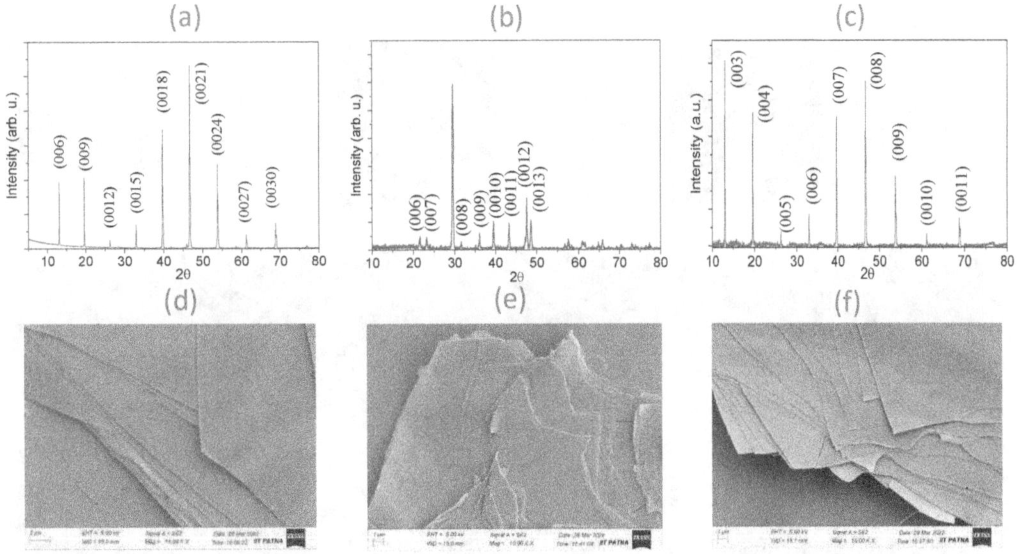

Figure 3.2: X-ray diffraction (XRD) pattern of (a) $MnBi_2Te_4$, (b) $MnBi_4Te_7$, and (c) $Mn_2Bi_2Te_5$. Inset figure depicts the optical micrograph of the MBT samples. Scanning electron microscopy (SEM) pattern of (a) $MnBi_2Te_4$, (b) $MnBi_4Te_7$, and (c) $Mn_2Bi_2Te_5$

$MnBi_2Te_4$ using precursors of Bi_2Te_3 (99.99% purity) and α-MnTe (99.9% purity) purchased from Sigma-Aldrich and Alfa Aesar, respectively. We mixed Bi_2Te_3 and α-MnTe in ratios of 1:1, 1:2, and 2:1 to synthesize $MnBi_2Te_4$, $MnBi_4Te_7$, and $Mn_2Bi_2Te_5$, respectively. We then made pellets from the powder and sealed them in an evacuated quartz ampoule using a home-built setup, as described in Chapter 2.

$MnBi_2Te_4$ was synthesized by heating the sample at 950°C for one day, followed by quenching in water. Subsequently, the sample was annealed at 565°C for 10 days to enhance the crystal quality. In the case of $MnBi_4Te_7$, a heat treatment was carried out by raising the temperature to 1000°C over 10 hours, maintaining it for 12 hours, and then cooling the furnace to 590°C over a period of 5 days. The furnace was then gradually cooled to 585°C over 3 days and held at that temperature for 8 days. Finally, the crystals were quenched in ice water. For $Mn_2Bi_2Te_5$, a similar procedure was employed as for $MnBi_4Te_7$, but the furnace was cooled down to 600°C over a period of 120 hours and kept at that temperature for an additional 12 hours before gradually cooling to room temperature over 3 days. The crystals were also quenched in ice water after the process.

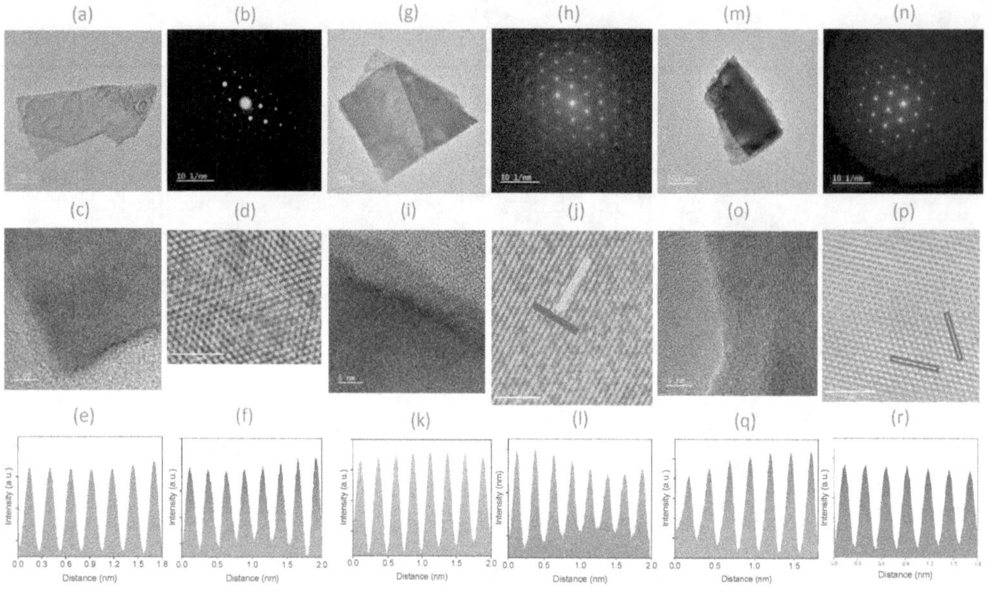

Figure 3.3: (a) TEM image of the mechanically exfoliated sheet of $MnBi_2Te_4$, (b) selected aread diffraction (SAED) pattern of the flake, (c) HRTEM image if the flake, (d) zoomed version of a area of the HRTEM image, (e) and (f) the the line profile obained from the selected area in Figure. 3.3(d). (g)-(l) and (m)-(r) represents similar plots for $MnBi_4Te_7$, and $Mn_2Bi_2Te_5$, respectively.

3.2.2 CHARACTERIZATION TECHNIQUES

The powder X-ray diffraction (XRD) patterns were acquired utilizing a PANalytical X-ray diffractometer with Cu-Kα radiation. The scanning electron microscope (SEM) images were captured using a scanning electron microscope. The Jeol JEM-2010 transmission electron microscopy (TEM) was utilized for the selected area diffraction (SAED) and high-resolution transmission electron microscopy (HRTEM) investigations. The Photoelectron Spectrometer was used to collect the X-ray photoelectron spectroscopy (XPS) spectra.

Magnetic property measurements were conducted using a Quantum Design vibrating sample magnetometer. Electrical transport measurements were performed in a CryoEdge Technology cryostat with a lowest attainable temperature of 8 K. For resistance and differential conductance measurements, a Keithley 6221 current source meter and 2182A nanovoltmeter setup were utilized.

3.2.3 RESULT AND DISCUSSIONS

To ascertain the phase and quality of the three MTIs crystals, Powder X-ray diffraction (XRD) was conducted. An inset image of the as-grown crystals of $MnBi_2Te_4$, $MnBi_4Te_7$, and $Mn_2Bi_2Te_5$ is included in Figure 3.2. The XRD pattern of the raw $MnBi_2Te_4$ single crystals (Figure 3.2(a)) exhibited sharp and intense peaks according to the (0 0 l), l = 3n, diffraction rule, indicating rhombohedral symmetry. In contrast, the XRD pattern of the raw $MnBi_4Te_7$ crystals showed comparatively broad peaks, with observed peaks following (0 0 l), l = 1. The XRD pattern of the raw $Mn_2Bi_2Te_5$ crystals demonstrated sharp and intense peaks, with observed peaks following (0 0 l), l = 1.

The present study displays scanning electron microscopy (SEM) images of exfoliated flakes of $MnBi_2Te_4$, $MnBi_4Te_7$, and $Mn_2Bi_2Te_5$ in Figure 3.2(d)-(f). The images reveal well-defined stratification in all exfoliated flakes, providing evidence for the successful synthesis of layered materials integrated by van der Waals forces. Additionally, Figure 3.3 presents the transmission electron microscopy (TEM), selected-area electron diffraction (SAED), and high-resolution TEM (HRTEM) images of the aforementioned samples. In the experiment, we initially exfoliated thin flakes of $MnBi_2Te_4$, $MnBi_4Te_7$, and $Mn_2Bi_2Te_5$ layers through mechanical means and transferred them onto a silicon substrate. We then carefully transferred the flakes to a TEM grid. All three samples exhibited hexagonal symmetry. The HRTEM image revealed the layered structure, represented as a contrast difference in the image. Upon zooming, we were able to observe atomic resolution images, from which we determined the lattice spacing (d_1 and d_2) derived from the line scan presented in Figure 3.3(e)-(f), (k)-(l) and (q)-(r). We estimated d_1 and d_2 to be 0.275 nm and 0.241 nm for $MnBi_2Te_4$, 0.271 nm and 0.274 nm for $MnBi_4Te_7$, and 0.247 nm and 0.274 nm for $Mn_2Bi_2Te_5$, respectively.

3.2.4 OXIDATION BEHAVIOUR AND STABILITY

X-ray photoelectron spectroscopy (XPS) measurements provided insights into the oxidation states of the MBT samples. The XPS survey spectrum confirmed the elemental composition.

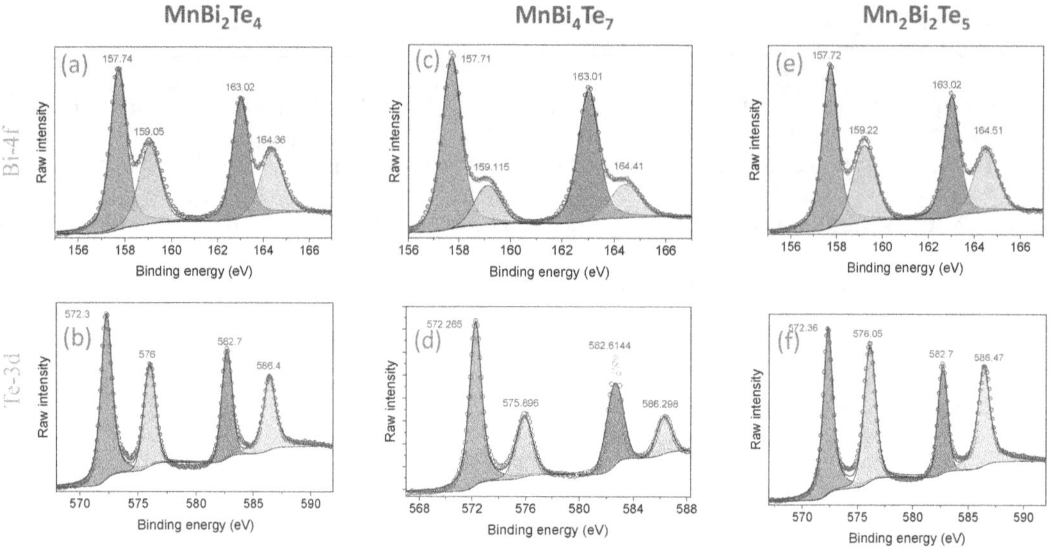

Figure 3.4: XPS spectra of (a) Bi-4f and (b) Te-3d level XPS acquired from the $MnBi_2Te_4$ surface without and with sputtering, respectively.(c)-(d) and (e)-(f) represents similar plots for $MnBi_4Te_7$ and $Mn_2Bi_2Te_5$ respectively.

The Bi-4f and Te-3d XPS spectra of the MBT samples were presented in Figure 3.4(a) and (b), respectively.

In the case of $MnBi_2Te_4$, the Bi-$4f_{7/2}$ and Bi-$4f_{5/2}$ peaks occurred at 157.74 eV and 163.02 eV, respectively, and were assigned to Bi^{3+} in Bi-Te bonds. The Bi-4f peaks due to Bi-O bonds appeared at 159.05 eV and 164.36 eV. The Te-3d spectrum exhibited two prominent peaks at 572.3 eV (Te-$3d_{5/2}$) and 582.7 eV (Te-$3d_{3/2}$) corresponding to Te2- in Bi-Te bonds and Mn-Te bonds, respectively. Two additional peaks at 576.0 eV and 586.4 eV were attributed to Te-O bonds, indicating oxidation of the $MnBi_2Te_4$ surface.

Table 3.1: Ratio of areas of Bi-$4f_{7/2}$/Bi-$4f_{5/2}$, Bi-O -$4f_{7/2}$/Bi-O -$4f_{5/2}$, Te-$3d_{5/2}$/Te-$3d_{3/2}$, Te-O -$3d_{5/2}$/Te-O -$3d_{3/2}$ peaks.

Sample	Area under Bi-$4f_{7/2}$	Area under Bi-$4f_{5/2}$	Ratio of area	Area under of Bi-O $4f_{7/2}$	Area under Bi-O $4f_{5/2}$	Ratio of area	Area under Te-$3d_{5/2}$	Area under Te-$3d_{3/2}$	Ratio of area	Area under Te-O $3d_{5/2}$	Area under Te-O $3d_{3/2}$	Ratio of area
$MnBi_2Te_4$	70462.5	52561.4	1.34	39987.9	31441.3	1.27	114152.8	56890.2	2	60708.9	61281.4	0.99
$MnBi_4Te_7$	92674.9	71401.6	1.3	23054	22078.3	1.04	106984.5	56543.9	1.89	44366.9	23105.9	1.92
$Mn_2Bi_2Te_5$	84402	60307.8	1.4	46427.8	36821.3	1.261	101742.2	56808.45	1.79	87149.41	82330.98	1.05

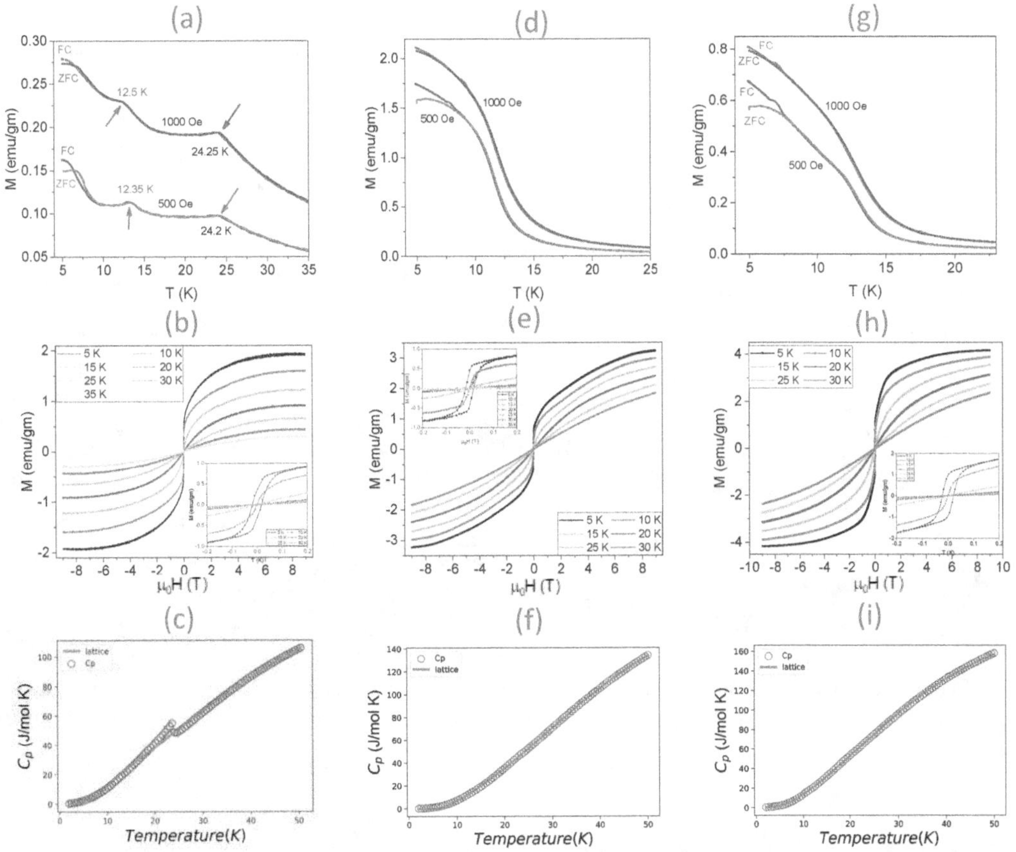

Figure 3.5: (a) Magnetization vs temperature plot (b) Magnetization vs magnetic field plot and (c) specific heat vs temperature for $MnBi_2Te_4$. (d)-(f) and (g)-(i) represents similar plots for $MnBi_4Te_7$ and $Mn_2Bi_2Te_5$.

For $MnBi_4Te_7$, the Bi-4$f_{7/2}$ and Bi-4$f_{5/2}$ peaks appeared at 157.71 eV and 163.01 eV, respectively, which were almost identical to those of $MnBi_2Te_4$. Bi-O 4$f_{7/2}$ and Bi-O 4$f_{5/2}$ peaks occurred at 159.115 eV and 164.41 eV. The Te-3d spectrum showed two major peaks at 572.265 eV (Te-3$d_{5/2}$) and 582.6144 eV (Te-3$d_{3/2}$) corresponding to Te2- in Bi-Te bonds and Mn-Te bonds, respectively. Two minor peaks at 575.896 eV and 586.298 eV were attributed to Te-O bonds. The ratio of the area under Bi 4$f_{7/2}$/Bi 4$f_{5/2}$, Bi-O 4$f_{7/2}$/Bi 4$f_{5/2}$ and Te-3$d_{5/2}$/Te-3$d_{3/2}$, Te-O 3$d_{5/2}$/Te-O 3$d_{3/2}$ are presented in Table.3.1.

Similarly, for $Mn_2Bi_2Te_5$, the Bi-4$f_{7/2}$ and Bi-4$f_{5/2}$ peaks occurred at 157.72 eV and 163.02 eV, respectively, which were almost identical to those of $MnBi_2Te_4$. Bi-O 4$f_{7/2}$ and Bi-O 4$f_{5/2}$ peaks occurred at 159.22 eV and 164.51 eV. The Te-3d spectrum exhibited two major peaks at 572.36 eV (Te-3$d_{5/2}$) and 582.7 eV (Te-3$d_{3/2}$)and two occured minor peaks at 576.05 eV and 586.47 eV are also visible in the Te-3d spectrum, which are attributed to Te-O bonds.

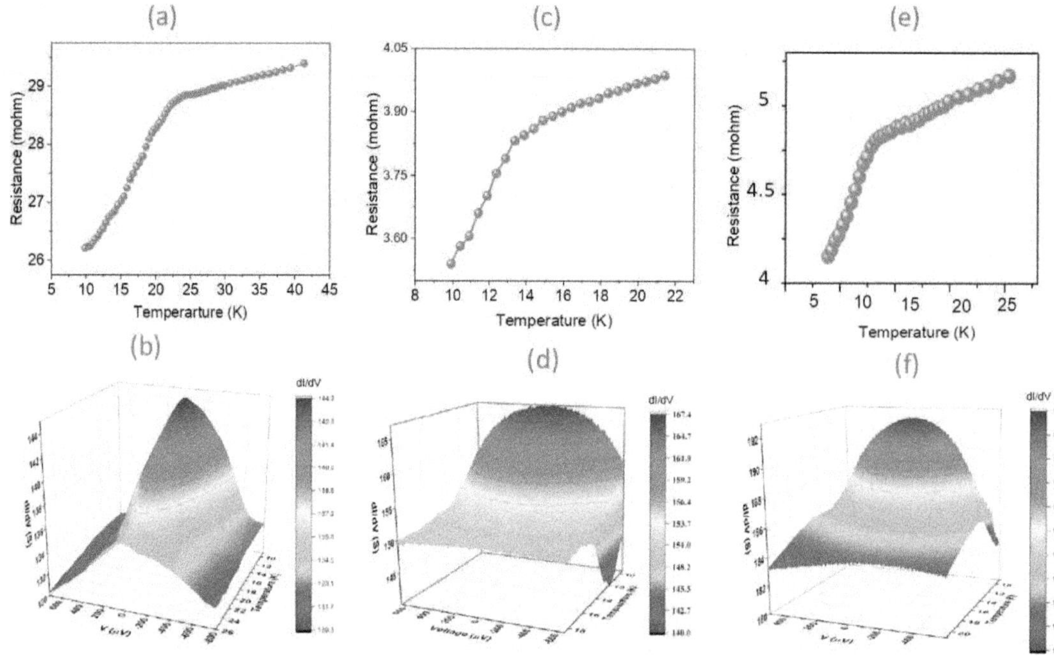

Figure 3.6: (a) Resistance vs temperature and (b) 3D plot of differential conductance as a function of temperature and voltage for $MnBi_2Te_4$ sample. (c)-(d) and (e)-(f) represents similar plots for $MnBi_4Te_7$ and $Mn_2Bi_2Te_5$ sample.

3.2.5 MAGNETIC MEASUREMENT

Figure. 3.5(a), (d) and (g) shows the temperature dependent zero field colled (ZFC) and Field cooled (FC) Magnetization vs Temperature plot for $MnBi_2Te_4$, $MnBi_4Te_7$ and $Mn_2Bi_2Te_5$ crystals measured at 500 and 1,000 Oe for the out-of-plane direction. It could be observed that for $MnBi_2Te_4$ transition point occured at two points, first one at 24.2 K and 24.2 K for 500 Oe and 1000 Oe. The second peak occurs at 12.35 K and 12.5K for 500 Oe and 1000 Oe. After the transition we indeed observed a downward trend in the M-T plot indicating the antiferromagnetic interaction manifesting particularly for 500 Oe applied magnetic field. In addition, as the sample is cooled, the ZFC data exhibit a decrease while the FC data show an increase, indicating the emergence of ferromagnetic (FM) domains. Unlike the characteristic plot of antiferromagnetic M-H plot of multiple-step features arising because the spin-flop transition or spin-flip transition, we observed a typical hysteresis loop for feerromagnetic materials at T=5K with coercivity of H_c = 0.047 T.On the other hand, for $MnBi_4Te_7$ and $Mn_2Bi_2Te_5$ no such peak was observed. In the specific heat vs temperature measurement (see Figure. 3.5(c), (f) and (i)). Here, we observed a sharp disontinuity in the plot is only apparent for $MnBi_2Te_4$ sample. Later, we performed magnetization vs applied magnetc field measurement(M-H) (see Figure. 3.5(b), (e) and (h)) in the range from -9T to 9T. Here, in the zoomed M-H plot for $MnBi_2Te_4$, $MnBi_4Te_7$ and $Mn_2Bi_2Te_5$ (see inset figure of Figure. 3.5(b), (e) and (h)) performed at 5K and 10K exhibited hyesresis pattern. In the specific heat vs temperature plot of $MnBi_4Te_7$ and $Mn_2Bi_2Te_5$, we did not find any prominent peak indicating a sharp phase transition.

3.2.6 TRANSPORT MEASUREMENT

A bulk sample measuring approximately 5 mm $\times$ 3 mm was subjected to transport measurement. To make contacts, silver epoxy was used, while Apiezon grease was used to attach the thin flake to the sample stage. The resistance versus temperature plot displayed a magnetic transition of the sample, with transition temperatures of 24 K, 13 K, and 10.1 K observed for $MnBi_2Te_4$, $MnBi_4Te_7$, and $Mn_2Bi_2Te_5$, respectively (Figure. 3.6.(a), (c) and (e)). Notably, the $MnBi_2Te_4$ sample displayed an upward turn in resistance prior to the transition temperature, followed by a downward turn. This behavior is attributed to spin scattering in antiferromagnetic topological insulators, which leads to a resistance versus temperature plot that first increases and then decreases, known as "re-entrant" resistivity. At low temperatures, surface states of MTI are highly spin-polarized due to the antiferromagnetic ordering of the lattice. With rising of temperature, thermal fluctuations begin to hinder the antiferromagnetic ordering, leading to the scattering of electrons by magnons in the surface states. Consequently, this electron scattering results in elevated resistance due to the decrease in spin polarization of the surface states.

Next we studied the three dimensional plot of differential conductance as a function of temperature and voltage has been presented for $MnBi_2Te_4$, $MnBi_4Te_7$, and $Mn_2Bi_2Te_5$ in Figure. 3.6.(b), (d) and (f). Here, we observed that for $MnBi_2Te_4$ plot the flat dome shaped region (denoted by colour 'Red' and 'Yellow' in the Figure. 3.6 indicates that the high conductivity region is highly sensitive to the bias voltage as we can see here, at T= 20 K at a bias volatge of $\approx 400\mu$V was able to diminish above feature. Here, also the dome became flat above 24K along voltage dircetion which signifies the transition from antiferromagnetic region to paramagnetic region. For $MnBi_4Te_7$, and $Mn_2Bi_2Te_5$ we observed a broader dome shaped region below corresponding transition temperature.

3.3 CONCLUSION

In this chapter, we presented a comprehensive study on the structural, magnetic and transport properties of three magnetic topological insulators, namely $MnBi_2Te_4$, $MnBi_4Te_7$, and $Mn_2Bi_2Te_5$. Our results indicate that all three samples exhibit prominent antiferromagnetic behavior, which was confirmed by both magnetic and transport measurements.

Furthermore, SEM and TEM imaging analyses revealed a layered nature of the samples, with highly coordinated atomic structures at the local level. Based on these observations, we can postulate that the supposed ferromagnetic behavior observed in $MnBi_4Te_7$ and $Mn_2Bi_2Te_5$ may be attributed to sample inhomogeneity, which can result in localized magnetic moments and thus lead to erroneous interpretations of the magnetic behavior. The present study provides a valuable contribution towards this goal and lays the groundwork for future investigations into the properties and applications of magnetic topological insulators.

4

EFFECT OF INTERLAYER TWIST ON ELECTRONIC, MAGNETIC, TRANSPORT, AND OPTICAL PROPERTIES OF $MNBI_2TE_4$/$CRGETE_3$ VAN DER WAALS HETEROSTRUCTURE

ABSTRACT

The concept of twistronics has recently gained significant attention due to its potential for controlling the electronic, magnetic, and optical properties of heterobilayers through manipulation of the twist angle between the layers. In this study, we investigated the electronic, magnetic, and optical properties of a CGT/MBT heterostructure for varying twist angles. Our results indicate that changes in the twist angle led to significant alterations in the band structure and density of states of the heterobilayer. Specifically, only two of the four twist angles studied (0° and 10.89°) exhibited band inversion. Furthermore, the optical properties of the heterostructure were found to be heavily influenced by the MBT layer, regardless of the twist angle. Monte Carlo simulations were also employed to estimate the exchange coupling between the layers. Our findings indicate that the system is antiferromagnetic at a twist angle of 0°, while at other angles, it exhibits ferromagnetic behavior.

4.1 INTRODUCTION

Following the first experimental confirmation of the existance of single-layer graphene [10], a myriad of two-dimensional (2D) materials have been synthesized. Although, single or several layer of 2D system have intriguing physical properties on their own, hetrostructure comprised of multiple 2D crystal layers bonded by Van der Waals force [55] can offer a plethora of opportuniries as they differ from the conventional three dimensional heterojunction. Here, each layer act as both material and interface, minimizing charge displacement. Nonetheless, charge transfers between layers can be quite substantial, resulting in huge electric fields and intriguing prospects in band-structure engineering [31]. The twist angle between in-plane lattices can break translational symmetry in the 2D system.[22, 56]. These offers an alternative pathway to manipulate the system properties like other approaches: doping[57, 58], straining [59], proximatizing with other materials. In special cases, the stacked heterostructures may have commensurate stacking, but it is more probable to get incommensurate structure. The twist angle can cause periodical lateral confinement and change the nature of the exciton in reciprocal space, making it a remarkable degree of freedom. The periodic superlattice that hosts this is called moiré patterns. In the most studied Van der Waals structure, twisted bilayer graphene (tBLG), depending on the twist angle superconducting state [21, 60], flat band [61], abnormal conductivity [62], tunable moire bands [63], orbital magnetoelectric effect [64], quantum anomalous Hall effect [65], Van Hove singularities [7]. Additionally, a wide variety of phenomena like moire excitation [66–68], atomic reconstruction [69], quantum anomalous Hall effect, strong electron correlation, photoluminescence [70, 71], topological gap [72], exciton Mott insulators [73] and quantum emitters [74] has been reported and predicted for twisted bilayer system. Now, the application of twist angle in controlling spin degree of freedom and engineering the magnetic properies is a innovative approach to study the area of topological magnetism [75, 76], moire bands [77], non-collinear magnetism [78]. According to theoretical research [79] and experimental studies [80, 81] on bilayer chromium tri-iodide, adjusting the stacking geometries from monoclinic to rhombohedral can cause magnetic transitions from antiferromagnetic to ferromagnetic order. Therefore, Moiré superlattices can cyclically modify the nature and magnitude of interlayer exchange coupling (ferromagnetic or antiferromagnetic) based on the twist angle. In our work, we investigated the electronic, magnetic and optical property of Van der Waals heterostructure of the monolayer of $MnBi_2Te_4$ and monolayer of $CrGeTe_3$ through Density Functonal Theory

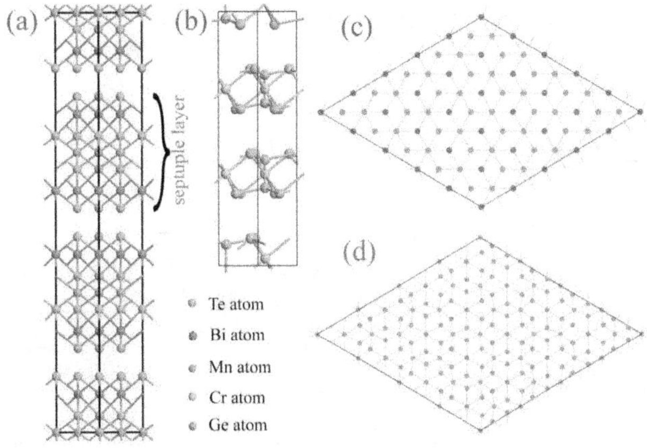

Figure 4.1: (a) Atomic structure of $MnBi_2Te_4$ with brown, purple, and light purple balls showing Te, Bi, and Mn atoms. (b) Atomic structure of $CrGeTe_3CrGeTe_3$ with brown, light blue, and light green balls showing Te, Cr, and Ge atoms. (c) 4x4 supercell of the monolayer of $MnBi_2Te_4$ and (d) 4x4 supercell of the monolayer of $CrGeTe_3$.

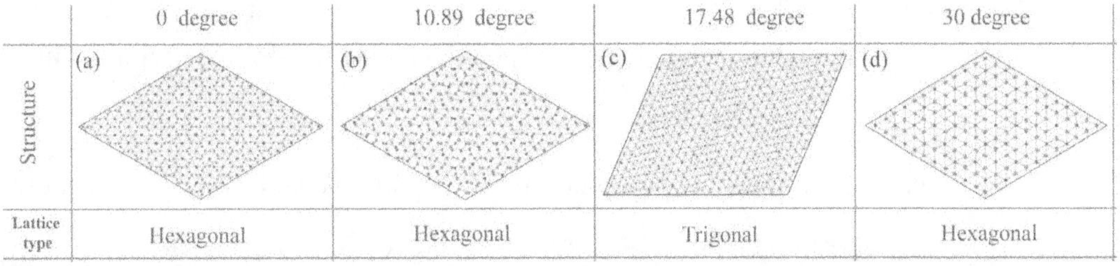

Figure 4.2: Top view of the MBT/CGT heterostructure with a twist angle of (a) 0°, (b) 10.89°, (c) 17.48°, and (d) 30° configurations. Here we showed 4 x 4 supercell for better visualization.

(DFT) calculations. $MnBi_2Te_4$ is an intrinsic magnetic topological insulator and $CrGeTe_3$ is an intrinsic ferromagnet.

The first intrinsic magnetic topologial insulator (MTI) vaildated the experimental and theoretical study is A-type antiferromagnetic topological insulator $MnBi_2Te_4$ (MBT). The synergy between magnetism and topology in a MTI) offers an exotic fiield to investigate quantized anomalous Hall (QAH) and magnetoelectric effect, axion electrodynamics, or Majorana fermions. MTIs are therefore very sought for applications in cutting-edge electronics and antiferromagnetic (AFM) spintronics. Similar to CrI_3, MBT films exhibited alternating FM/AFM interlayer magnetic order depending on the odd/even numbers of layers. The monolayer of MBT exhibits D_{3d} symmetry and possesses a triangular lattice structure. The monolayer comprises of seven atoms that are arranged in a Te-Bi-Te-Mn-Te-Bi-Te sequence, which follows an ABC stacking .

Table 4.1: The estimated bandgap for CGT, MBT monolayer and their heterostructures for SOC (SCAN functional), SOC (PBE functional)+DFT-D3 Grimme correction and SGGA+U method. The values are presented in electron volts (eV).

	SOC+SCAN		SOC+DFT-D3		SGGA+U	
	Direct	Indirect	Direct	Indirect	Direct	Indirect
MBT_{ml}	0.0005	0.0005	0.0125	0.0125	1.119	0.956
CGT_{ml}	1.35	0.676	0.912	0.362	0.952	0.555
$\theta_r = 0°$	0	0	0 eV	0 eV	0 eV	0 eV
$\theta_r = 10.89°$	0.0062	0.0061	0	0 eV	0.4138	0.4138
$\theta_r = 17.48°$	0	0	0	0	0	0 eV
$\theta_r = 30°$	0.0158	—	0.0011	—	0.3471	0.1765

We chose four heterostructures where the twist angle (θ_r =) between the layers are: 0°, 10.89°, 17.48°, and 30° (reason why this four angle was chosen is described in supplementary article). Among the four structures, three are hexagonal and one (17.48°) is triclinic. For θ_r = 0°, we observed a Moiré pattern in the lattice configuration. 10.89° did not exhibit any pattern. 17.48° on the other hand exhibited a stripe pattern whereas 30° showed a hexagonal pattern. It has been shown that Perdew-Burke-Ernzerhof (PBE) density functional misses most vdW interactions and barely binds layered materials [82, 83]. On the downside, for magnetic property calculation SCAN performed worse compared to the PBE.Therefore, for electronic calculation we preferred spin-orbit coupled meta-generalized gradient approximation (SOMGGA) approximation. For magnetic calculations we used spin-polarized generalized gradient approximation and the Hubbard-U approximation (SGGA+U). Spin-orbit coupled generalized gradient approximation (SOGGA) with DFT-D3 Grimme correction (SOGGA+DFT-D3) was also done for comparison.

4.2 COMPUTATIONAL DETAILS AND SYSTEM DESCRIPTIONS

We utilized the interface builder package of Atomistix Toolkit (ATK) software to construct a unit cell consisting of the cleaved $MnBi_2Te_4$ and $CrGeTe_3$ monolayers along (001) direction. Henceforth, we shall refer to the monolayer of $MnBi_2Te_4$ (MBT) as MBT_{ml} and the monolayer of $CrGeTe_3$ (CGT) as CGT_{ml}. We kept the lattice constant of $MnBi_2Te_4$ unchanged while $CrGeTe_3$ was stretched to fit the unit cell. We constructed four different heterostructures with

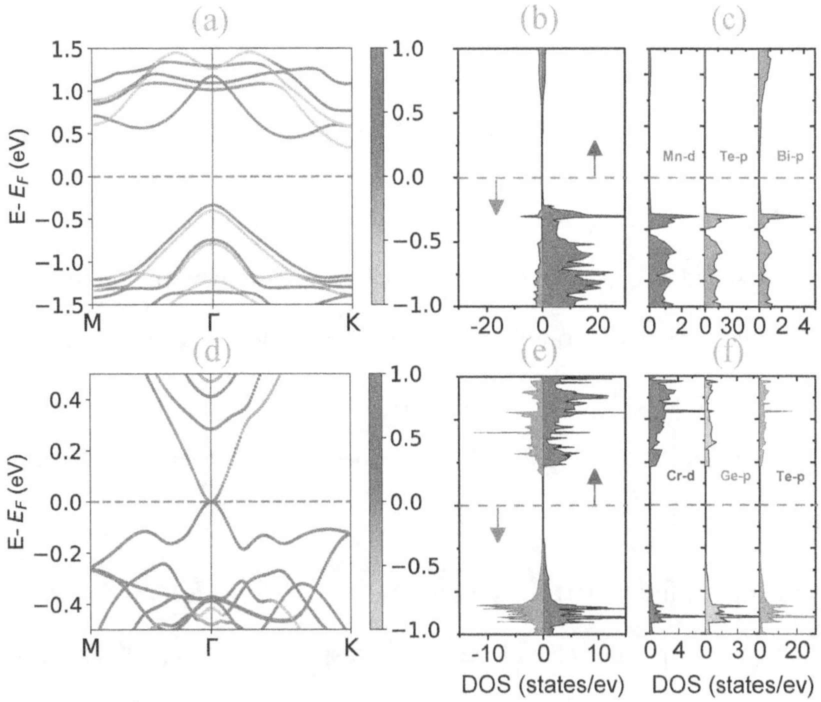

Figure 4.3: (a) Band structure obtained using the meta-GGA functional SCAN, incorporating spin-orbit coupling. (b) Spin-projected density of states, where the down arrow signifies the down spin, and the 'up' arrow denotes the up spin. (c) Atomic orbital-projected density of states for the MBT monolayer. Panels (d) to (f) depict analogous plots for the CGT monolayer.

a twist angle $\theta_r = 0°$, 10.89°, 17.48°, and 30°.The strain on the CGT layer and 4.26%, 3.12%, 5.27%, and 5.39% for $\theta_r = 0°$, 10.89°, 17.48°, and 30° respectively.

During the calculation, the LCAO basis set was utilized with a cutoff energy of 2993.25 eV. A Monkhorst-Pack k-point mesh of $9 \times 9 \times 1$ was employed throughout, and to eliminate any interactions with periodic images of the bilayer, a vacuum of 15 Å was added in the z-direction. In the SGGA+U method, which was utilized to account for the 3d electrons of Cr and Mn, the effective onsite coulomb interaction parameter (U) was set to 1 and 3 eV, respectively, in accordance with previous research [84]. Both SGGA+U and SOC+DFT-D3 calculations employed the Perdew-Burke-Enzerhof parametrization for describing electron core interaction. For SOMGGA calculations, Strongly-Constrained and Appropriately-Normed (SCAN) functional, along with norm-conserving pseudopotentials was used.

4.3 RESULTS AND DISCUSSION

4.3.1 ELECTRONIC CHARACTERISTIC OF TWISTED HETEROSTRUCTURE

MBT_{ml} and CGT_{ml} both belong to the P$\bar{3}$m1 space group and have optimized in-plane lattice constant of 6.83 Å and 4.33 Å. The lattice mismatch varies depending on the twist angle. To determine the energetacally favorable twisted bilayer system, we calculated the formation energy, $E_f = -(E_{het}-E_{CGT_{ml}}-E_{MBT_{ml}})$, where E_{het}, $E_{CGT_{ml}}$, $E_{MBT_{ml}}$ is the total energy of the twisted heterostructure, CGT_{ml} and MBT_{ml} respectively. A negative E_f implies that the heterostructure is stable.

First we calculated the bandstructure and density of states (DOS) for isolated MBT_{ml} and CGT_{ml} layer. The spin projected band strcture, spin projected DOS and atom projected DOS for MBT_{ml} and CGT_{ml} calculated through SCAN functional has been presented in Figure. 4.3(a)-(c) and Figure. 4.3(d)-(f) respectively. CGT_{ml} has a direct bandgap of 1.35 eV and indirect bandgap of 0.676 eV under (see Figure. 4.3.f). The indirect bandgap obtained by SOC+DFT-D3 and SGGA+U method are 0.362 eV and 0.555 eV for CGT monolayer. Now, in previous studies, CGT monalyer is reported to have an indirect bandgap of 0.91 eV [85] derived using hybrid functional HSE06. So overall, electronic calculation performed using SOC + SCAN method produced results comparable to the result reported by using hybrid functional.

As depicted in Figure 4.3(a), the direct bandgap of MBT_{ml} is measured to be 0.5 meV. Additionally, we have estimated direct bandgap of 12.5 meV and indirect bandgap of 0.956 eV utilizing SOGGA+DFT-D3 and SGGA+U formalism. Now, the reported bandgap of MBT_{ml} is 0.70 eV [86] and 0.750 $\pm$ 0.10 eV [87] which is much higher than the result we obtained through SOC+SCAN and SOC+DFT-D3 method. On the other hand, SGGA+U severely overestimated the bandgap.

The spin projected bandstructure of the MBT/CGT heterostructure with $\theta_r = 0^o$ is presented in Figure.4.4.(a). Here, we have observed that the conduction band minima exhibit a minimal overlap with the Fermi level. Specifically, the band structure of MBT_{ml} revealed the presence

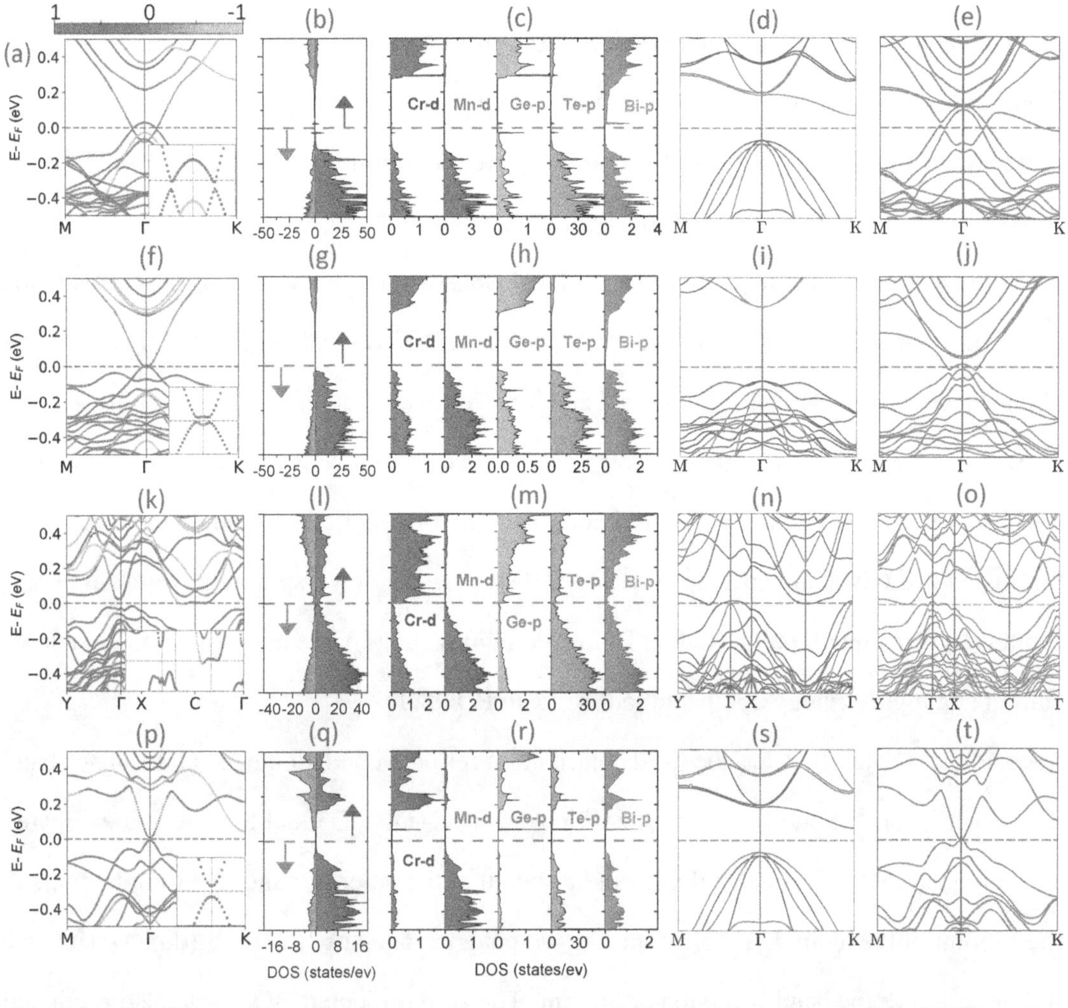

Figure 4.4: (a) Spin projected bandstructure, (b) spin projected density of states (obtained by using SCAN functional), Bandstructure obtained by (c) GGA functional with spin polarization and Hubbard U correction, and (d) GGA functional with spin-orbit coupling and DFT-D3 Grimme correction for 0° configurations. (e)-(h); (i)-(l); (m)-(p) and (q)-(t) represents similar plots for 10.89°, 17.48°, and 30° configuration.

of a Dirac cone shape, which exhibited a bifurcation into two distinct Dirac cones in the regions between M-Γ and Γ-K. The zoomed version (see inset of Figure.4.4.(a)) illustrates band inversion happening between the lowest conduction band with the highest valance band thus displaying the spin up behaviour around the Γ point. On the other hand, the highest valance band had band inversion with the second highest valance band also which lead to the highest valance band having three region raging from spin of -1, 0 and 1 as we move away from Γ in both Γ-M and Γ-K direction. In the spin projected density of states, we observed two spikes both for up-spin and down-spin where the amplitude for the up-spin is higher. Apart from those spikes we observed a flat region from -0.08 eV to 0.23 eV. From the oribtal projectd DOS we can deduce that Te-*p* orital (l=1) mostly contributed most for both condction band and valance band near fermi energy. From SOC+DFT-D3 and SGGA+U calculation, we obtained an indirect bandgap of 0.362 eV and 0.555 eV (see Figure.4.4.(d) and Figure.4.4.(e)). As we increased the twist angle to 10.89° we observed an indirect bandgap of 6.1 meV. Here we observed a clear demonstration of band inversion of conduction band and valance band but instead of CBM showing up spin and VBM showing down spin here VBM showed *s* orbital (l= 0) aroung Γ point. In the PDOS (see Figure. 4.4.(f)), we observed both spin down started at a higher energy compared to θ_r= 0°. In PDOS Te-
textcolorred*p* orital (l=1) has the most contribution for both condction band and valance band near fermi energy. For, θ_r = 17.48°there SCAN, SOC+DFT-D3 and SGGA + U estimated metallic state. At 30° twist angle, it can be seen that the valence band maximum occurs at the Γ-point of the moiré Brillouin zone and we got a bandgap of 15.8 meV (direct). Here we did not observe the band inversion at Γ point. The spin projected DOS state also predicted a sizeable gap. In SOC+DFT-D3 and SGGA + U we got a bandgap of 1.1 meV (direct) and 176.5 meV (indirect) respectively. One interesting observation is that the bandstructure obtained for θ_r = 0° and 30° are same only exchanging the spin of the corresponding band.

Projecting the wavefunctions onto the spherical harmonics reveals that the p orbitals of the Te atoms make up the majority of the atomic orbitals, with modest contributions from the *d* orbitals of the Chromium and *p* orbitals of the Bismuth atom around the Fermi level.

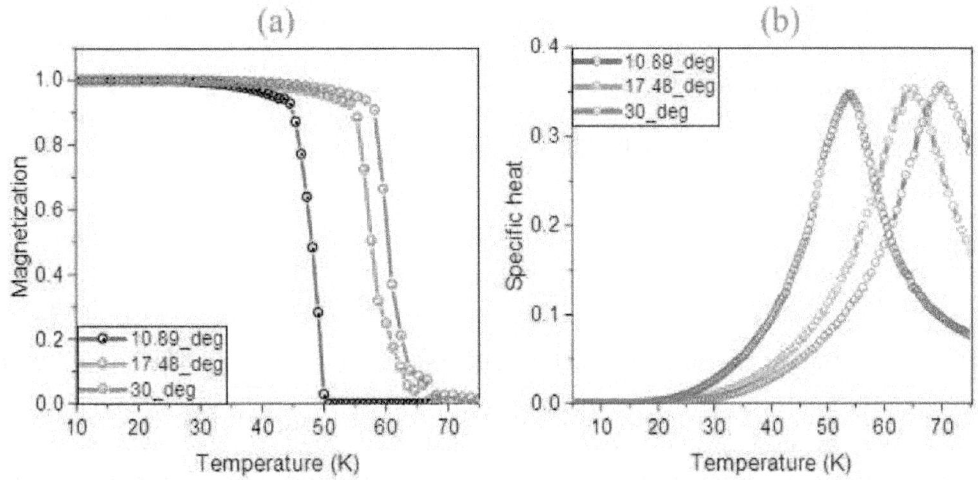

Figure 4.5: Magnetization vs tempertaure plot calculated by Monte Carlo Simulation for (a) CGT and MBT monolayer and (b) heterostrure with twist angle 10.89°, 17.48°, and 30° respectively.

4.3.2 MAGNETIC PROPERTIES

To achieve the most stable magnetic ordering, two ferromagnetic (FM_1 and FM_2) and two antiferromagnetic (AFM_1 and AFM_2) orders were considered. Now, the exchange energy can be expressed by

$$\Delta E = E_{FM} - E_{AFM} \tag{4.1}$$

where E_{FM} and E_{AFM} are the total energy corresponding to FM and AFM configurations respectively. In order to estimate the Curie temperature, the Monte Carlo method based on the 2D Ising model was employed. This stochastic method utilizes random numbers and probability statistics to investigate problems. A theoretical model description is used to estimate the Hamiltonian of the system. To begin, a ferromagnet with extremely high uniaxial anisotropy is postulated, which may be characterised by the Ising model, in which

$$\hat{H} = -\sum_{<i,j>} J_{ij} S_i . S_j \tag{4.2}$$

where, S_i signifies the spin at lattice site i pointing parllel or antiparallel to the "easy axis", the exchange coupling J_{ij} accounts only for nearest-neighbor interactions and $\hat{H}$ is the external magnetic field. Now, J_{ij} can be written as

$$J_{\text{ij}} = -\frac{\Delta E}{2NS^2} \tag{4.3}$$

where, N is the number of nearest neighbours and S is the spin. J$>$0 signifies the FM ordering and J$<$0 signifies the AFM ordering. For the estimation of Curie temperature, we have used the ground state energy obtained from the SGGA+U method. SCAN functional usually underestimates the curie temperature.

A 16×16 supercell of the unit cell was taken as the basis for the Monte Carlo simulation which was ran upto 10^5 iteration for better accuracy. For the monolayer MBT and CGT layer, we obtained a Curie temperature of 12.5 K and 60 K which is closer to the experimental value of the bulk MBT and CGT. Now, among the heterostructure, the configuration with 0° twist angle showed AFM interlayer coupling whereas other twist angles showed FM coupling between the CGT and MBT layer. For, 10.89°, 17.48°, and 30° we obtained a curie temperature of 15 K, 15 K, and 61 K (see Figure. 4.5).

4.3.3 OPTICAL PROPERTIES

We employed DFT-based analysis to investigate the optical response that results from electron transitions occurring between the first three valence bands located below the Fermi level and the first three conduction bands situated above it. The primary focus of this section is to check the probability of such transitions occurring across various symmetry points within the 1st Brillouin zone. Additionally, we aimed to identify the corresponding maximum energy of the transitions to gain an insight of the optical properties of the system under investigation. Notably, we employed the 'SCAN' exchange-correlation potential, a semi-empirical functional, to carry out all the optical property calculations presented in this section, given its suitability for the computation of optical characteristics. Subsequently, we evaluated the absorption coefficient, refractive index, and optical conductivity of the twisted

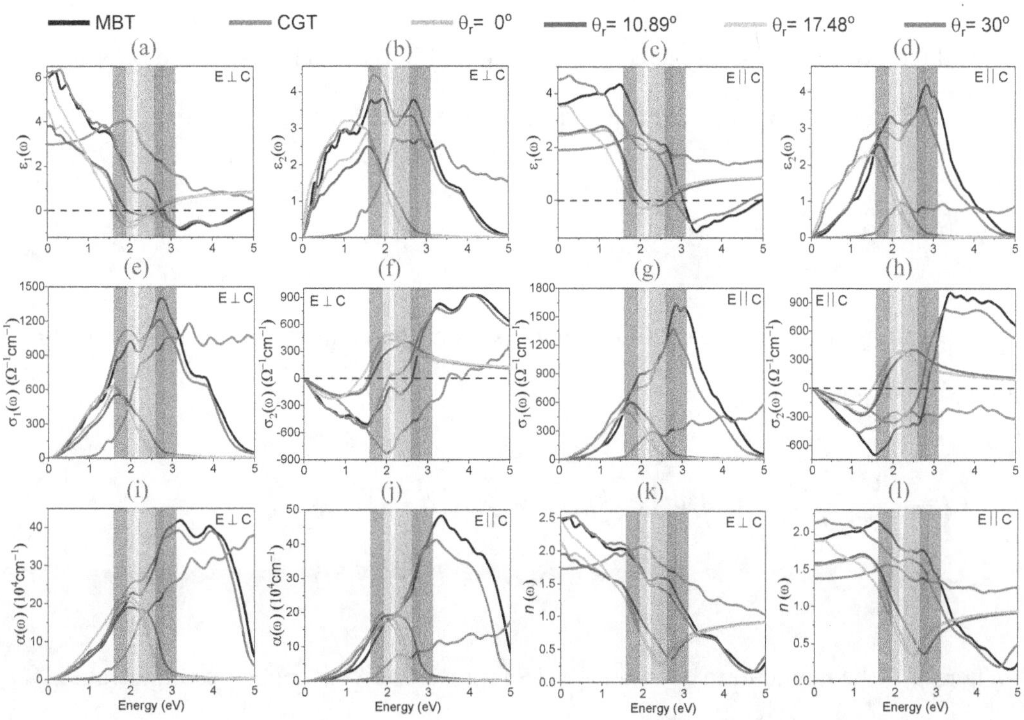

Figure 4.6: (a) The real and imaginary part of the dielectric constant vs energy, (b) Absorption coefficient vs energy (c) refractive index vs energy, and (d) real and imaginary part of the optical conductivity as a function of energy. (e)-(h) represent similar plots for twisted heterostructure with $\theta_r = 0°$. (g)-(l), (m)-(r), (s)-(x) represents similar plots for heterostructure with $\theta_r = 10.89°$, 17.48°, and 30°.

Table 4.2: Static real part of dielectric function $\epsilon_1(0)$ and static refractive index ($n(0)$) along E⊥c and E||c

	E⊥c		E‖c	
	$\epsilon_1(0)$	$n(0)$	$\epsilon_1(0)$	$n(0)$
MBT_{ml}	6.01	2.45	3.60	1.90
CGT_{ml}	2.98	1.73	1.89	1.38
$\theta_r = 0°$	4.53	2.123	2.43	1.56
$\theta_r = 10.89°$	3.80	1.95	2.50	1.8
$\theta_r = 17.48°$	5.98	2.44	3.53	1.88
$\theta_r = 30°$	6.19	2.49	4.5	2.12

heterobilayer systems, namely MBT_{ml}, CGT_{ml}, and MBT/CGT, across the photon energy range of 0-5 eV. The complex dielectric function can be described as

$$\epsilon(\omega) = \epsilon_1(\omega) + i\epsilon_2(\omega) \tag{4.4}$$

where ϵ_1 and ϵ_2 are the the real and imginary parts of the dielectric function. The imaginary part can be computed using

$$\epsilon_2 = \frac{e^2\hbar^2}{\pi m^2\omega^2}\Sigma_{nn'} = \int_k d^3| < \vec{k}_n|\vec{p}|\vec{k}_{n'} > |^2[1 - f(\vec{k}_n)] \\ \delta(E_{\vec{k}n} - E_{\vec{k}n'} - \hbar\omega) \tag{4.5}$$

Where $\vec{p}$ is the momentum operator, $|\vec{k}_n >$ represents eigenfunction of eigenvalue, $f(\vec{k}_n)$ is the Fermi distribution function. The real part of the dielectric function can be derived from the Kramers–Kronig transformation

$$\epsilon_1(\omega) = 1 + \frac{2}{\pi}\int_0^\infty \frac{\epsilon_2(\omega')\omega' d\omega'}{\omega'^2 - \omega^2} \tag{4.6}$$

The function under consideration describes the mechanism of light propagation within a given material. A positive value of the real part of the dielectric function (ϵ_1) signifies the light absorption characteristics of the material at a given frequency. Peaks in the imaginary part of the dielectric function (ϵ_2) indicate the allowed electric-dipole transitions between the

Table 4.3: Static real part of dielectric function $\epsilon_1(0)$and static refractive index E⊥c and E||c

	E⊥c			E||c		
	$\alpha_{max}(\times10^4)$	n_{max}	σ_{1max}	$\alpha_{max}(\times10^4)$	n_{max}	σ_{1max}
MBT_{ml}	41.76 (3.21 eV)	2.49 (0.20 eV)	1396.44 (2.75 eV)	48.21 (3.34 eV)	2.15 (1.55 eV)	1625.29 (2.85 eV)
CGT_{ml}	31.97 (5.0 eV)	2.06 (1.99 eV)	1176.56 (3.46 eV)	18.85 (5.0 eV)	1.56 (1.78 eV)	576.06 (5.0 eV)
θ_r =0°	21.96 (1.93 eV)	2.12 (0 eV)	615.87 (1.63 eV)	19.29 (2.19 eV)	1.62 (1.21 eV)	608.66 (1.71 eV)
θ_r =10.89°	21.96 (1.93 eV)	1.96 (0.95 eV)	556.87 (1.69 eV)	19.38 (2.15 eV)	1.71 (1.96 eV)	596.94 (1.75 eV)
θ_r =17.48°	21.96 (1.93 eV)	2.44 (0 eV)	638.37 (1.63 eV)	17.49 (1.91 eV)	1.89 (0.27 eV)	493.04 (1.63 eV)
θ_r =30°	39.24 (3.17 eV)	2.53 (0.31 eV)	1211.38 (2.71 eV)	41.20 (3.20 eV)	2.17 (0.29 eV)	1358.91 (2.78 eV)

valence and conduction bands. In this study, we have considered two polarization directions, E||C and E⊥C. Figure 4.6(a)-(b) presents plots of the real (ϵ_1) and imaginary (ϵ_2) parts of the dielectric function for E⊥C polarization of the electric field, for MBT_{ml}, CGT_{ml}, and all the twisted heterobilayer configurations. Figure 4.6(c)-(d) presents similar plots for E||C polarization. From these plots, we have extracted the values of the static part of the real dielectric constant ($\epsilon_1(0)$) for MBT_{ml}, CGT_{ml}, and twisted heterostructures with θ_r = 0°, 10.89°, 17.48°, and 30° for E⊥C and E||C polarization directions. These values are tabulated in Table 4.2. Here, found $\epsilon_1(0)$ for MBT_{ml}, CGT_{ml} to be 6.01 and 2.98 for E⊥c and 3.60 and 1.89 for E||c respectively. For the twisted heterobilayers, θ_r = 30° exhibited highest $\epsilon_1(0)$. Additionally, we observed a gradual increment in the $\epsilon_1(0)$ for twisted heterostructure as we increase the θ_r when E||c. When the real part of the dielectric function (ϵ_1) drops below zero, it indicates that the incident photon beam is attenuated due to the dissipation of energy into the medium, resulting in metallic behavior. On the other hand, the drop of $\epsilon_1(\omega)$ from its maximum value can be associated with the increase in the imaginary part of the dielectric function ($\epsilon_2(\omega)$), which suggests inter-band transitions. The static value of real dielectric constant [$\epsilon_1(0)$] is inversely related to the energy bandgap E_g by;

$$\epsilon_1(0) = 1 + (\frac{\hbar\omega}{E_g})^2 \tag{4.7}$$

Based on equation 4.7 presented above, it can be inferred that a higher bandgap value corresponds to a lower value of $\epsilon_1(0)$. Empirical evidence confirms that a lower bandgap value in a surface system results in a significantly reduced $\epsilon_1(0)$. T*he highest peak of* $\epsilon_2(0)$ *is located at ≈1.60, 1.50, 1.30 and 0.45 eV for* θ_r *= 0°, 10.89°, 17.48°, and 30°.*

Optical Conductivity: The real and imaginary components of the optical conductivity σ_{real} and $\sigma_{\text{imaginary}}$ are given by

$$\sigma_{\text{real}} = \frac{E\epsilon_2}{4\pi\hbar} \tag{4.8}$$

$$\sigma_{\text{imaginary}} = \frac{E(1-\epsilon_1)}{4\pi\hbar} \tag{4.9}$$

The real and imaginary part of the frequency-dependent optical conductivity is plotted in Figure. 4.6.(d), 4.6.(e)-(f) (for E⊥c), and 4.6.(g)-(h) (for E||c) for for MBT_{ml}, CGT_{ml} and twisted heterostructure with θ_r = 0°, 10.89°, 17.48°, and 30°. Here we observed, CGT monolayer demonstrating low conductivity in the infrared region, whereas very high conductivity in both visible and UV regions. For, twisted heterostructure with θ_r = 0°, 10.89°, 17.48°, and 30°, the highest optical conductivity was observed for θ_r = 30°.

Absorption coefficient: The absorption coefficient (α) can also be derived from the the dielctric function by the following relation

$$\alpha(\omega) = \frac{2\omega(|\epsilon(\omega)| - Re\epsilon(\omega))^{1/2}}{c} \tag{4.10}$$

The absorption coefficient is a fundamental quantity that enables the quantification of the attenuation of light intensity as it traverses a material. This coefficient is contingent upon both the wavelength of the incident light and the dielectric constant of the material. Now, For, CGT_{ml} the absorption coefficient is high in the UV region, and for the MBT_{ml} absorption coefficient is high between 2.7 – 4.3 eV which lies between the UV region. Now, here the absorption coefficient for 'xx' and 'yy' direction coincides with each other, and 'zz' direction is higher compared to the 'xx' and 'yy' direction. For, for the herostructure with θ_r= 30, it roughly follows the trend of MBT monolayer except from the attenuation of the 'zz' component in the 2.7- 4.3 eV region. The point at which the positive tangent drawn on the $\alpha(\omega)$ cut the x-axis may be considered as an optical band gap. From the plot, we deduced that 'xx' and 'yy' component has very low optical bandgap. 'zz' component although higher than 'xx' and 'yy' component is still for all the twisted heterostructure.

Refractive index: Figure. 4.6(k)-(l) illustrates the calculated refactive index (n) vs energy. Typically, the refractive index provides insight into the degree of light refraction as it enters a medium. The refractive index can be calculated as

$$n = \sqrt{\frac{\epsilon_1 + \sqrt{{\epsilon_1}^2 + {\epsilon_2}^2}}{2}} \tag{4.11}$$

The static refractice index (n_0) for MBT_{ml}, CGT_{ml} are 2.45, 1.73 for E⊥c and 1.90, 1.38 for E||c respectively. For the twisted heterostructure the highest value of n_0 has been observed for θ= 30° (2.49 for E⊥c and 2.12 for E||c). For E||c we observed a gradual increase in the value of n_0 as we increase the θ_r.

In Table. 4.3 we have tabulated the highest value of n (n_{max}). The highest for MBT_{ml}, CGT_{ml} are 2.49,2.06 for E⊥c and 2.15, 1.56 for E||c respectively.

4.4 CONCLUSION

Twistronics has gained huge momentum in recent years as they offer a unique perspective of manipulating the electronic, magnetic, and optical chracteristics of the heterobilayer concerning the twist angle between the layers. Now, here we attempted to estimate the mentioned properties for CGT/MBT heterostructure for different angles. As we observed, with angle there were drastic changes in the band structure and DOS in the heterobilayer. Among 4 systems only two (0° and 10.89°) exhibited the signature of band inversion here. In the optical property estimation, we found out the optical properties of the heterostructure to be heavily influenced by the MBT layer irrespective of the twist angle. From the Monte

Carlo simulation, we also estimated the exchange coupling between the layers and found out the at 0° twist angle the system is AFM in nature whereas for other angles it's FM in nature.

5

PROXIMITY INDUCED COLOSSAL CONDUCTIVITY MODULATION IN PHOSPHORENE

ABSTRACT

Phosphorene is a promising single-elemental two-dimensional layered semiconductor with huge potential for future nanoelectronics and spintronics applications. In this work, we investigate the effect of an organic molecule (benzene) in the close proximity of a phosphorene nanoribbon. Our extensive calculations reveal that the semiconducting nature of phosphorene remains unaffected as a result of the molecular adsorption while the transport properties go through drastic changes. Under the influence of dopant atoms and external strain, colossal changes in the conductivity are observed, with a maximum enhancement >1500%. This effect is pretty robust against (i) variation of the system size, (ii) the type, location, and concentration of dopants and (iii) the nature and magnitude of the external strain. Furthermore, we demonstrated how a gate voltage can be used to fine tune the enhanced conductivity response in a field-effect transistor (FET) structure. Our results provide direction for phosphorene-based nanoelectronics in applications such as sensing, switching where a higher level of conduction can offer better resolution, a higher on:off ratio, and superior energy efficiency.

5.1 INTRODUCTION

Similar to other Van der Waals materials, Phosphorene is a single atomic layer of black phosphorus with semiconducting properties and a layered structure featuring strong in-plane

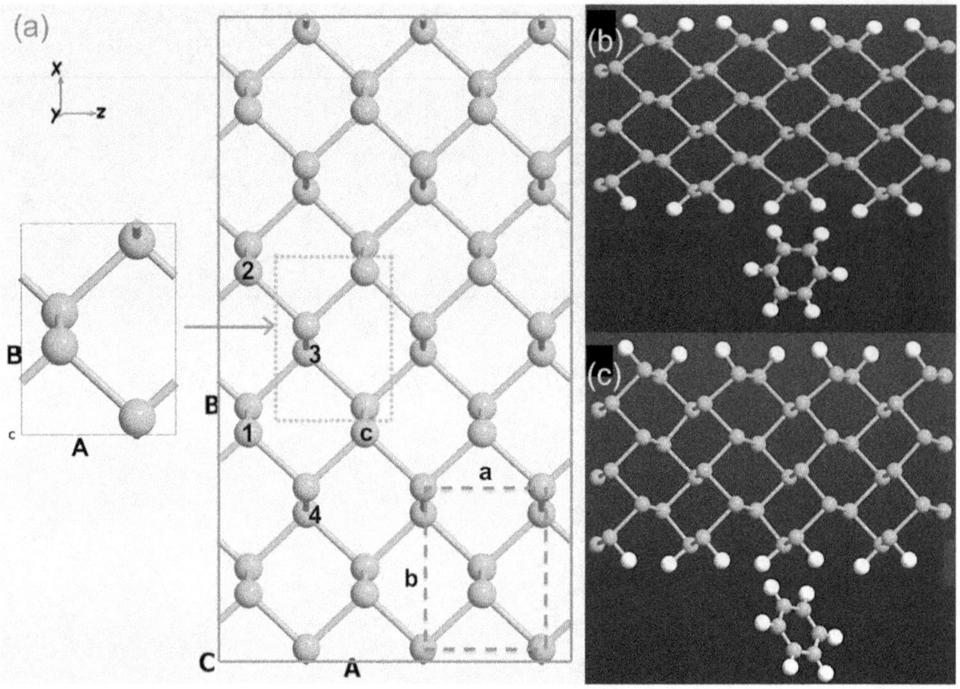

Figure 5.1: Schematic of the top view of (left) unit cell of 2D phosphorene and (right) 3×4 supercell of 2D phosphorene where the two dotted boxes are the unit cells with **a** and **b** as the lattice vectors. Various doping locations are marked by C (centre doping) and 1, 2, 3, 4 for the locations for edge doping with with those numbers of dopant atoms. APNR in the presence of Benzene molecule : (b) molecule and layer lying in the same plane, (c) molecule is tilted with respect to the APNR plane.

bonds and weak out-of-plane Van der Waals interactions. After the first successful isolation of mono and few layers phosphorene from fulk phosphorous crytals using mechanical exfoliation in 2014 [88], phosphorene stimulated a wave in 2D materials research activity owing to its semiconducting nature. Phosphorene boasts exciting features, including a layer-dependent bandgap that spans from 0.3 eV to 2.0 eV. [89–92], low spin orbit coupling [93], ambipolar transport [29], large ON/OFF ratio [28, 94] etc. Additionally, the high degree of in-plane anisotropy leads to the angle dependent transport [95, 96] and optical property. Furthermore, excellent mobility of 10^3 $cm^2V^{-1}s^{-1}$ [97] and drain current modulation of the order of 10^5 [94] was observed in 10 nm thick phosphorene sheet. At room temperature, it is much higher in comparison to the transisition metal dichalcogenides (TMDs). The above mentioned properties makes phosphorene an desirable candidate for future nano and opto elctronic devices like Field-effect transistor (FET), photodetectors, solar cells, terahertz imaging, batteries etc.

The elevated surface to volume ratio makes 2D materials highly responsive towards neighbouring molecule as demonstrated in graphene [98] and carbon-nitrogen compounds [99]. This work employs first-principles based self consistent DFT calculations to investigate the effect of proximity of Benzene (C_6H_6) molecule on the electronic and transport properties of an armchair Phosphorene nanoribbon (APNR). Benzene lies at the heart of organic chemistry and is widely used in various industries due to its easy availability. Using the NEGF formalism, we investigated the APNR's current-voltage characteristics in the presence and absence of Benzene. Additionally, we explored the impact of system size, doping type and location, and uniaxial strains on conductivity response, and how gate voltage can fine-tune conductivity in realistic FET geometry.

5.2 COMPUTATIONAL DETAILS

Calculation of the electronic structure and geometry relaxation have been carried out by DFT utilizing the Atomistix ToolKit (ATK). The exchange-correlation energy was assessed using the Perdew-Burke-Ernzerhof exchange-correlation functional within the Generalised Gradient Approximation (GGA) with an energy cut-off limit of 180 Ry. The reciprocal space of the Brillouin Zone was sampled using a $27 \times 27 \times 1$ Monkhorst-Pack k-grid. A distance of 15 Å has been maintained along the 'C' axis to minimize intyerlayer interaction. The APNR structures (in pristine and adsorbed conditions) were structurally relaxed until the force on each atom was less than 10^{-3} eV/Å in the equilibrium condition.

The NEGF-combined Density Functional Theory methodology was used to conduct all transportation calculations in the two-probe geometry. We calculated the current by utilizing the Landauer-B$\ddot{u}$ttiker formula that we have presented in Eqn. 2.20.

5.3 SYSTEM DESCRIPTION

The lattice constants of the unit cell of Phosphorene are **a** = 3.3136 Åand **b** = 4.3763 Å, where **a** and **b** denote the distances between two successive P atoms along the zigzag and armchair directions, respectively, as shown in Fig.5.1.The bond length along the zigzag

Table 5.1: The summary of the abbreviations used in this chapter

Abbreviation	Details	Abbreviation	Details
APNR	Armchair Phosphorene Nanoribbon	A_{mn}	APNR with length n [times the primitive lattice parameter **b**] and width m [primitive lattice parameter **a**] (general)
P(subscript)	Pristine	A(subscript)	Adsorbed
A_{34}	APNR with m=3, n=4 (general)	A_{34P}	APNR with m=3, n=4 (pristine structure)
A_{34A}	APNR with m=3, n=4 (adsorbed configuration)	A_{54P}	APNR with m=5, n=4 (pristine structure)
A_{54A}	APNR with m=5, n=4 (adsorbed configuration)	A_{34CSi}	APNR with m=3, n=4, centre doped with Si (no adsorption)
A_{34CSiA}	APNR with m=3, n=4, centre doped with Si (adsorbed configuration)	A_{34CS}	APNR with m=3, n=4, centre doped with S (general)
A_{34E4Si}	APNR with m=3, n=4, edge doped with 4 Si atoms (general)	A_{34E2Si}	APNR with m=3, n=4, edge doped with 2 Si atoms (general)
A_{34E2S}	APNR with m=3, n=4, edge doped with 2 S atoms (general)	A_{34E4S}	APNR with m=3, n=4, edge doped with 4 S atoms (general)
A_{34E1Si}	APNR with m=3, n=4, edge doped with 1 Si atom (general)	A_{34E3S}	APNR with m=3, n=4, edge doped with 3 S atoms (general)

direction containing the in-plane hinge angle of 95.370° is 2.24 Å while the connecting bond lengths along the armchair direction is 2.26 Å. We designated an $m \times n$ sized APNR as A_{mn} which has dimensions : m times **a** along the zigzag direction and n times **b** along the armchair direction. In the present work, we have considered a H-edge passivated 3×4 supercell of APNR as our central structure, which is abbreviated as A_{34P} in pristine structure (no doping and defect) and A_{34A} as the (benzene) adsorbed configuration while A_{34} is used for general use.

5.4 RESULT AND DISCUSSION

5.4.1 PRISTINE SYSTEM

The electronic band structure of A_{34} in unpasivated, passivated and benzene adsorbed condition is illustrated in Fig. 5.2, which is observed to be a direct bandgap semiconductor. Compared to the unpassivated system, an increment in bandgap is observed from 0.88 eV to

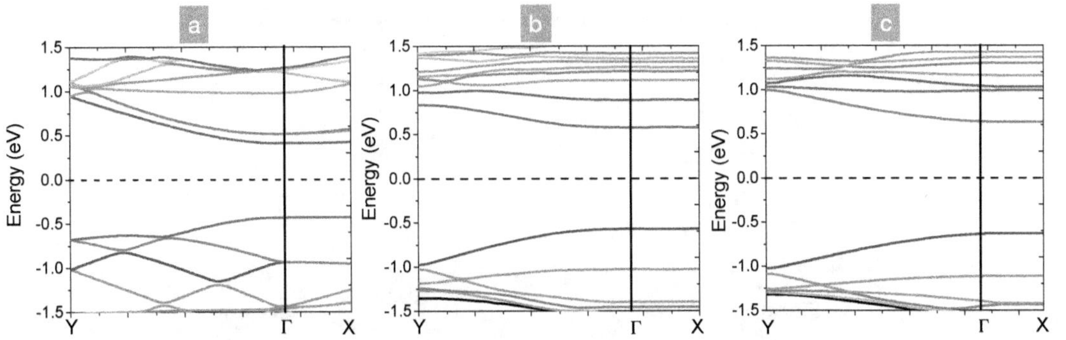

Figure 5.2: Band structure of A_{34} in (a) unpassivated, (b) H-edge passivated and (c) after absorbing benzene molecule configurations.

1.24 eV due to H-passivation. The origin for this increment can be traced by comparing the band structures between these two scenarios.

In Fig.5.2.(b),we can see that the hydrogen-passivation caused increase in bandgap of A_{34}. After absorbing a Benzene molecule, the bandgap of A_{34} changes to 1.26 eV (Figure.5.2.(c)), but molecular adsorption does not affect the semiconducting properties of the APNR. The experimentally reported band gap for monolayered phosphorene is between 0.98 - 1.45 eV [28, 29, 38], which is comparable to our estimated value.

The schematic of the two probe device for transport calculation is shown in Figure 5.3:(a). The benzene molecule was adsorbed to the side of the APNR in a measurement geometry. The planar configuration (Figure. 5.3) was found to have lower energy compared to the tilted configuration in several tested configurations. The planar configuration is the preferred geometry. At zero bias state, there is no flow of current as the density of states in the electrodes are the same. When the applied voltage increases above 0.9 V, which approximately matches the band gap of A_{34} current starts flowing. In the molecule adsorbed configuration, the IV-curve's general form demonstrates a gapped structure, similar to what was noticed in the initial situation.

The current-voltage (IV) characteristics of the A_{34} system were investigated, as presented in Figure.5.3.(b). At zero bias, no current was observed due to the identical density of states in both electrodes. A non-zero current was observed when the applied bias exceeded 0.9 V, which corresponds roughly to the band gap of A_{34}. The overall shape of the IV-curve for the system with the attached molecule resembled that of the pristine case, indicating that

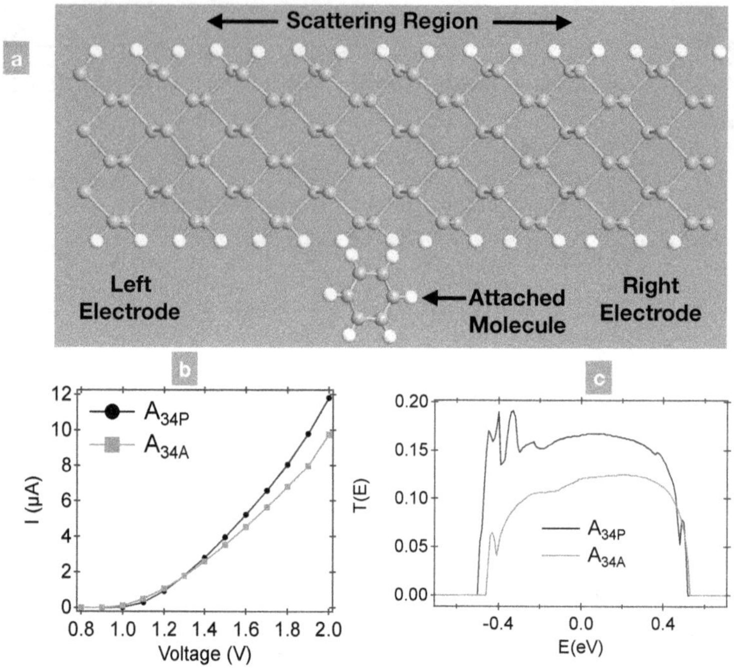

Figure 5.3: (a) Schematic of an APNR in 2-probe geometry for IV-calculations with attached Benzene molecule, (b) Current-voltage relationship of A_{34} in pristine and adsorbed configuration, (c) Corresponding transmission spectrum at 2.0V of applied bias.

the molecule did not significantly alter the gapped structure. However, a slight reduction in current was observed at around 1.2 V and beyond, which was more prominent at higher applied biases. This can be attributed to the reduction in the local density of electronic states along the conduction pathways, caused by the attachment of the molecule. Consequently, the available conduction paths and transmission were slightly reduced, leading to reduced current/conduction. The transmission behavior, as shown in Figure.5.3(c), supported this explanation, with the transmission value within the energy range of -0.5 eV to 0.5 eV being noticeably greater in the pristine setup than in the adsorbed configuration. The significant difference in the IV characteristics at higher voltages suggests that APNR is sensitive to the presence of organic objects, and this sensitivity can be quantified by measuring the difference in current at a particular applied bias. A quantitative estimation can be done using the modulation factor (η) defined at a given bias V as,

$$\eta(V) = \left|\frac{I_A(V) - I_U(V)}{I_U(V)}\right| = \left|\frac{\Delta I(V)}{I_U(V)}\right| \quad (5.1)$$

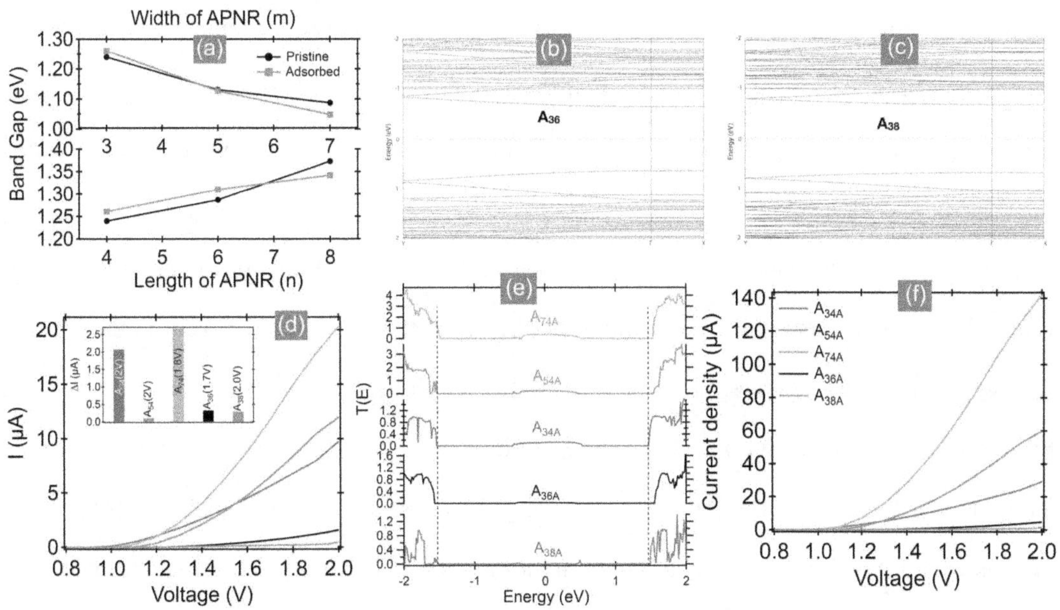

Figure 5.4: (a) Dependance of the Bandgap with the length (n) and width (m) of APNR in pristine and adsorbed configuration. The bandstructure of the H-edge passivated APNR for different lengths : (b) A_{36} and (c) A_{38}. (d) Current-voltage relationship of A_{mn} in the adsorbed configuration and (inset) maximum ΔI for these cases, (e) Transmission spectrum at 2.0V applied bias for these adsorbed configurations respectively. Current density (defined as current per unit width) of the APNR in different adsorbed configuration as given in Figure 5.4(d).

where I_A and I_U are the currents in adsorbed and unadsorbed configuration of the APNR respectively.

Next, we have checked the impact of system size on the electronic and transport characteristics in the presence of the molecule. The size dependence of the bandgap as function of length (n) and width (m) is illustrated in Figure 5.4(a). With an increase in width, the band gap gets reduced which is a consequence of quantum confinement effect. Additionally, an increase in the length (n) results in an increase in the bandgap. Also, the bands become flatter (Figure 5.4(b)-(c)) as the length increases. It is a result of increased scattering along the ribbon length causing the transmission probability to decrease drastically, which implies an increase in effective mass and hence the flatter bands. However, the band dispersions remain more or less same with m variation. In both the length and width variation, the band gap for the adsorbed system follows the similar trend as that of its pristine counterpart.

The IV-relationships in the adsorbed configuration for various combinations of m, n are illustrated in Figure 5.4(d). With an increase in m, the current at higher bias gets enhanced while the reverse trend is observed with an increase in n i.e the reduction in current. The highest current is observed when the band gap is the lowest. With an increase in the length of the ribbon, the overall value of transmission decreases as also shown in Figure 5.4:(e). For A_{34A}, A_{54A} and A_{74A} a non-zero transmission peak around 0 eV is visible which almost disappears for A_{36A} and A_{38A}. With an increase in m, the central window of transmission stays more or less unchanged as represented through the dotted lines. But the actual value of transmission increases manifold at other energies. As the calculated current is the integral sum of transmission, hence this gets reflected through the IV-patterns (current density in Figure 5.4:(f). While the width is kept fixed, but length is increased - the carriers have to travel a larger path and hence probability of scattering increases and transmission get reduced. On the contrary, for a fixed length an increase in the ribbon width can add additional transmission pathways that can result in an enhanced conduction. While looking at the change in current (ΔI) as a result of the adsorption, a measurable difference is observed for all the configurations tested here as displayed in Figure 5.4(d) (inset). A maximum in $\Delta I \sim 2.7\ \mu A$ is observed for A_{74P} which is about 29.5% higher than the value estimated for A_{34P}. Such values of ΔI are experimentally measurable and well-above the experimental noise floor ($\sim$ pA) at room temperature and much higher than the typical values reported for Phosphorene [100, 101].

The effect of the width of the nanoribbon in the transport property can be understood from the current density behaviour, which is defined here as the calculated current per unit width of the supercell (m) of the APNR. The total current calculated for APNR of different supercell sizes is given in Figure 5.4(d). Here in Figure 5.4(f), the current is scaled by m as given in Figure 5.4(d). Increase in the width of APNR adds additional transport channels for conduction which leads to steepest slope of the IV-curve for A_{74A} which has the largest width and the reverse is observed for A_{38A}. We have compared it quantitatively by comparing current differences (ΔI) at 2V applied bias. Between A_{34A} and A_{54A}, current density increases by 30.65 μA while between A_{54A} and A_{74A}, the enhancement is 82.41 μA, which is almost 2.7 times larger between the two cases. Comparing between A_{34A} and A_{36A}, the current density gets reduced by 24.42 μA and the same between A_{36A} and A_{38A} is 3.29 μA, which is a reduction by a factor of 7.4 between the corresponding cases. This clearly demonstrates the drastic effect of the decrease in the width of APNR in the reduction of its conductance.

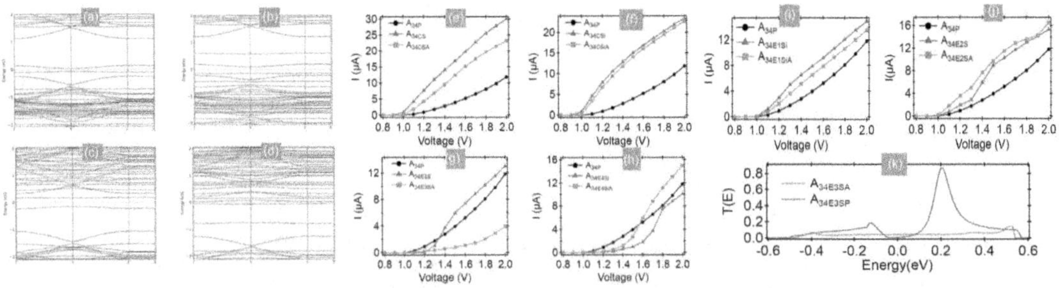

Figure 5.5: The bandstructure of the APNR in various doping conditions (a) edge doped with 2 Si (A_{34E2Si}), (b) edge doped with 4 Si (A_{34E4Si}), (c) edge doped with 2 S (A_{34E2S}), (d) edge-doped with 4 S atoms (A_{34E4S}). IV-characteristics of A_{34} in doped configurations with (e) centre-doped with S, (f) centre-doped with Si, (g) edge-doped with 3 S atoms, and (h) edge-doped with 4 Si atoms. The red, blue and black lines represent the undoped, doped and adsorbed configurations respectively. IV-characteristics in various doped configurations of the APNR : (i) edge-doped with 1 Si and (j) edge-doped with 2 S atoms. Symbol meaning : Black (undoped/pristine), Blue (Doped), Red (Doped and Adsorbed). Transmission spectrum of the edge-doped APNR with 3 Sulphur atoms (E3S) at an applied bias of 2.0 V in the presence and absence of the molecule.

In terms of modulation, $\eta \sim 150\%$ is observed for A_{38P}, which indicates the large change of the transport properties of APNR can be brought in the presence of the molecule. This property can thus be well-utilised for designing a nano-sensor made of Phosphorene. With a change of the edge structure, it will be interesting to study the behaviour of zigzag nanoribbon under identical ciscumstances. In earlier works involving graphene nanoribbon, it was observed that transport behaviour gets modulated independent of the edge structures [102]. The shape of the nanoribbon determines the transport pathways for conduction and any modification to this can perturb the other.

5.4.2 EFFECT OF DOPING

To explore the impact of doping on the electronic and transport characteristics of the APNR, two different doping strategies were employed. Silicon was used as p-type dopant while Sulphur as n-type dopant. Doping was carried out at specific sites for both types, with the dopant atom inserted either at the center (center doping) or at the edge (edge doping). In our calculation edge doping concentrations have been increased gradually by sequentially replacing the numerically marked sites (see Figure. 5.1) with 1(1.56%); 2(3.125%); 3(4.59%) and 4(6.25%) dopant atoms. They are named as C (centre doped with 1 atom) and E1-E4 (edge doped with 1-4 atoms respectively). The nomenclature used to define these doped configurations are illustrtated in Table. 5.1. To avoid undesirable doping of the electrodes, the

Table 5.2: A comparison of the maximum conductivity modulation (η) of the APNR in various doping configurations

Doping Configuration	η(Si)	η (S)
C1 (1.56%)	84.24 %(1 V)	83.57% (1 V)
E1 (1.56%)	39.29% (1.1 V)	90.77% (1.1 V)
E2 (3.13%)	90.32% (1.1 V)	142.07% (1.1 V)
E3 (4.59%)	206.44% (1.1 V)	569.80% (1.2 V)
E4 (6.25%)	228.07% (1.6 V)	84.94% (1.1 V)

edge doping of A_{34P} is restricted to a maximum of four dopant atoms.

The IV-curves for A_{34P} centre doped with Sulphur is illustrated in Figure. 5.5(e). In all the 3 configurations, significant current starts flowing when the applied bias crosses 0.9V, which is a signature of a semiconductor with a sizeable bandgap. Compared to the pristine configuration, the value of current stays significantly higher in the doped geometry and the difference gets enhanced ($\Delta I_{max} = 18.16\mu A$) with an increase in the bias. In the proximity of the benzene molecule, the IV-pattern follows a similar trend as that of the doped case but a marked difference between the two lines is significant for the entire bias region. In this doped configuration, a maximum value of $\eta \sim 83.57\%$ is observed and a maximum $\Delta I = 6.8\mu A$. In a similar manner pronounced effect of Si-doping at the centre can be seen from the IV-characteristics in Figure 5.5:(f). With an increase in the applied bias above the gap size of APNR, current in the doped configuration gets highly enhanced compared to its pristine counterpart with a maximum $\Delta I = 10.9\mu A$ at 2V. In the presence of benzene, the difference in the current between the two configurations is clearly visible.

For the edge-doped configuration with 3 S and 4 Si atoms, the IV-characteristics are shown in Figure 5.5(g-h) respectively. For both types of dopants, the onset voltage (V_{onset}) at which finite current starts flowing in the system gets enhanced in the doped configuration compared its pristine counterparts. For Si-doping in Fig. 5.5(h), $V_{onset} \sim 0.9$V in the pristine structure while in the doped geometry, $V_{onset} \sim 1.2V$. This trend is present for S-doping in Fig. 5.5(g), but the difference between the onset voltage between the pristine and doped configuration increases with an increase in the doping percentage. With an increment in the applied bias in Fig. 5.5(h), current starts rising monotonically in the doped configuration both in the presence and absence of the benzene molecule and clear difference between the current(s) indicates that edge-doping has a more pronounced effect for Si (Fig. 5.5(i-j)). This leads to a huge enhancement η of 228.07% and a significant $\Delta I \sim 5\mu A$ at high voltages.

For S-doping at the edge in Figure. 5.5(g), a pronounced difference in the current was observed as a result of the proximity effect with a η = 569.80% and a maximum $\Delta I = 9.1\mu A$. The large change in the current suggests the enhanced proximity influence of the C_6H_6 molecule in this APNR. In the edge doped APNR, additional carriers are locally more available near the edge region which is in closer proximity to the benzene molecule. This leads to a larger change in the transmission as presented in Figure. 5.5(k). The disappearance of the transmission peak around the Fermi level in the presence of Benzene significantly reduces the integrated sum of T(E) over the entire bias range leading to a huge reduction of current. For various doping configurations, the values of η are tabulated in Table 5.2 which are significantly large independent of the doping type and configuration. The general trend suggests that both p/n-type dopants are useful for the conductivity modulation of APNR. As doping in a semiconductor introduces additional charge carriers for conduction, which for a 2D material with higher surface sensitivity results in an enhanced charge transfer between the layer and the molecule and conductivity changes. To better the value of η, edge doping is more effective which for Si increases monotonically with an increase in the doping percentage. This offers additional tuneability in the conduction response after the adsorption of an organic molecule.

The presence of Benzene molecule has not been found to affect the bandstructure of the doped APNR (both for Si or S doping). However, the transport properties gets affected to a great degree and showed varying characteristics depending upon the site and concentration of doping as the dopant states are induced near the Fermi level of the central scattering region. It is expected that in the case of A_{34P} where the current decreased on adsorption, similar circumstance would occur for the doped APNR until sufficient delocalised energy states are provided by the dopant atoms and in our study we also observed similar situation. We have noticed decrement in current after absorption of Benzene molecule when the APNR is doped upto 2 Si but when the system is doped with 3 and 4 Si atoms respectively current increased after the absorption of Benzene molecule. On the other hand for Sulphur doped APNR, fall in current is observed when the system is doped with 1 S atom (both centre and edge doped) and rise in current is observed after the system is doped with 2 or 4 S atom which satisfy our claim.

In the pristine configuration, the centre-doped APNR clearly transports magnitude of current higher than the other doped ribbons. This is due to the fact that in an H-edge passivated APNR the H-P bonds are stronger and the edge states are located deep in the bands [103]. The CBM (conduction band minima) and the VBM (valance band maximum) are contributed by the atoms in the central region while centrally doped Si creates dopant state in the Fermi level. Consequently, the major part of the current flows through the central pathways as also observed from the transmission analysis. Henceforth to magnify the current values further, the delocalised states created by the centrally doped Si is preferable compared to edge doped configurations.

5.4.3 INFLUENCE OF STRAIN

To investigate the influence of external strain on the conductivity of the APNR, electronic and transport properties were studied in the pristine and adsorbed configurations. The percentage uniaxial strain is defined using the following equation : $S = 100\% \times (a - a_0)/a_0$ where $a_0(a)$ is the lattice parameter in the unstrained (strained) structure of the APNR. In this work, we have covered a significantly large strain range of S = -15% to +15%. Within this region of strain, the gap size of the APNR stayed within a range of 0.8 - 1.3 eV (see Figure 5.6(a)). In the adsorbed condition, no major changes in the band gap was observed except a small difference at S = 6%. This suggests that the semiconducting nature of the material do not get affected on benzene adsorption in the strained configuration. The APNR was found to be stable within the elastic limit for a maximum applied strain of S = 30%.

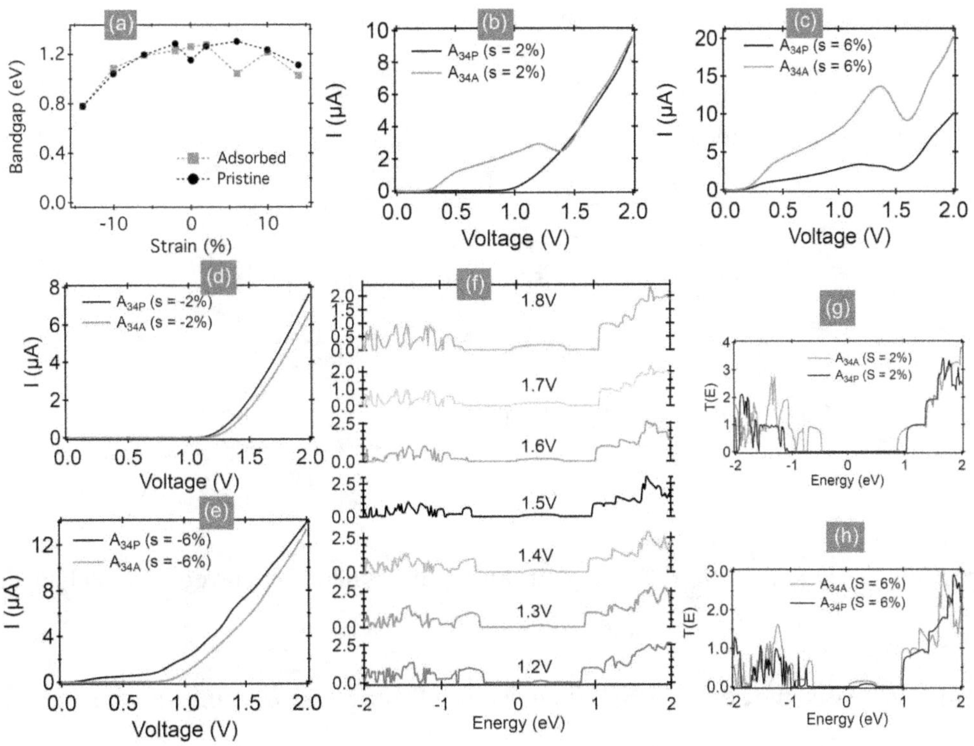

Figure 5.6: (a) Variation of bandgap with applied strain (%) in the Pristine and adsorbed configurations of the APNR. IV-response of A_{34} in pristine and adsorbed configurations under (b) 2%, (c) 6%, (d) -2% and (e) -6% applied strain. (f) Transmission spectrum of A_{34A} under S=6% at different bias voltage.

The semiconducting nature of the APNR is visible from the IV-behaviour of A_{34P} at $S = 2\%$ as shown in Figure 5.6(b). On adsorption, the current starts flowing at a much smaller bias compared to A_{34P} and above 1.45V, the current traces a similar path as that of its pristine counterpart. At $S = 6\%$, the difference in the IV-charactristics in Figure 5.6(c) between the pristine and adsorbed configurations are much more pronounced over the entire range of applied bias. In the adsorbed configuration, above 0.2V, current starts increasing with an increase in the applied bias with a current peak at 1.36V followed by a minimum at 1.6V - above which it increases sharply at higher voltages. This kind of conductance oscillations have been observed in Phosphorene and other 2D materials [102, 104] which can be explained using the changes in the transmission behaviour as shown in Figure 5.6(f). Similar peak and valley regions are weakly visible in the pristine configuration, but the overall amplitude of current oscillations is relatively less. In the compressive strain region [Figure 5.6(d-e)], the gapped electronic structure of the APNR is noticeable from the IV-responses and the current in the adsorbed configuration is lower than the pristine configuration over the entire bias

Table 5.3: A comparison of the maximum conductivity modulation (η) of the APNR at various values of strain percentages

Strain	η	Strain	η
2%	1527.81 (1.0 V)	- 2%	85.90 (1.2 V)
6%	365.44 (1.5 V)	- 6%	86.77 (0.9 V)
10%	232.5 (0.2 V)	- 10%	81.59 (0.8 V)
14%	70.32 (1.1 V)	- 14%	42.85 (0.1 V)

range. This is in contrast to the tensile strain regime where the current gets enhanced on adsorption.

As we increased the applied strain (in tensile and compressive regimes), the APNR starts conducting at a lower voltage than the unstrained APNR in both absorbed and unabsorbed configurations. For S = 6% non-zero current is measured at 0.2 volt and for both S = 10% and 14% conduction started at an astonishingly small bias of 0.1 volt), in spite of having a larger band gap. Similar trend is observed in the compressive strain region, where for S = -6%, the current starts flowing at 0.1V for the pristine case. This disparity in the relation of large bandgap and low bias voltage for conducting current is the consequence of electrodes becoming semi-metallic when strained. The reasoning behind this occurence is that under the application of an in-plane strain, the layer gets stretched horizontally. This enhances the in-plane bond length between the P-atoms and a reduction of the out-of-plane bond length. As a result, the overlap of $3p_x, 3p_y$ orbitals between neighbouring P atoms gets reduced, while the $3p_z$ contribution gets enhanced in respective cases. When the in-plane lattice sites are widely separated, this diminishes the scattering probability by increasing the scattering time due to this reduced orbital overlap. This results in the current hike when the applied strain is increased upto a certain extent. In the compressive strain region, the hopping probability gets enhanced with a higher degree of overlap between the $3p_x, 3p_y$ orbitals which can explain the onset of the current at lower bias.

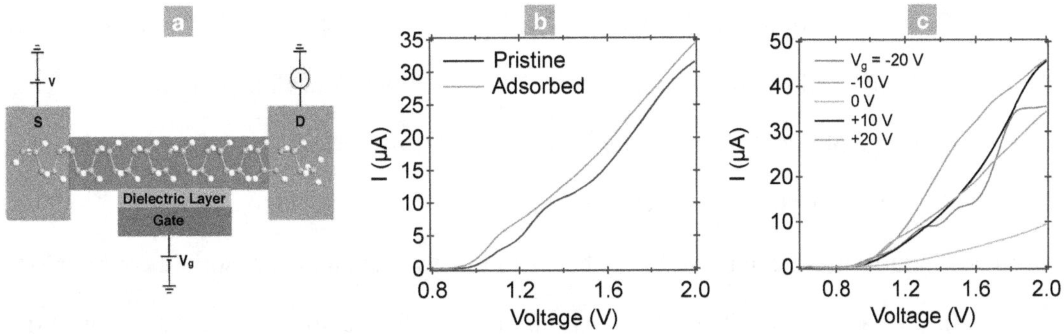

Figure 5.7: (a) APNR based FET structure with a backgate, (b) IV-characteritics of A_{34} at V_g = 20V in pristine and adsorbed configurations, (c) IV-response in the adsorbed configuration (A_{34A}) at various values of V_g.

The conductivity changes obtained for different strain configuration is listed in Table. 5.3 which is significantly large for the entire region of strain studied here. Overall, η is higher in the tensile regime compared to the compressive cases. At S = 2%, a colossal value of η = 1527.8% was observed which on enhancement of tensile strain stays high with a value of 365.44% at S = 6%. Within the Landauer's formalism, such high value of η can be explained by comparing the transmission behaviour of APNR before and after the adsorption is illustrated in Figure 5.6(g) for S=2% at 1V of applied bias. Between the energy range of -0.46 eV→-1.07 eV and 0.87eV→ 1.02 eV, transmission is mostly absent in the pristine system while it is non-zero for the adsorbed case. Compared to the pristine case, T(E) is significantly higher for the adsorbed case upto an energy of -1.5 eV. Similar differences in transmission was also observed for S = 6% at 1.5V of applied bias (Figure 5.6(h)) which explains the origin of high value of η for these cases. The value of η in the compressive strain regime stayed over 80% upto S = -10%. Such level of unprecedented conductivity modulation has not been observed in Phosphorene earlier which suggests that the application of strain can be a very effective way of achieving enhanced conduction in Phosphorene.

5.4.4 EFFECT OF A GATE VOLTAGE

To comprehend the impact of gate voltage on conduction behaviour, the transport proprties of APNR were examined in a FET architecture, as seen in Figure. 5.7(a). Via a dielectric layer, a metallic gate connects the APNR to the structure. The dielectric constant was determined to be $\epsilon_r = 4.2$, which is equivalent to that of SiO_2. In an all Phosphorene FET, the Source (S) and Drain (D) electrodes are likewise assumed to be composed of Phosphorene.

In the presence of a gate voltage, the IV-pattern retains the semiconducting character of the APNR in the FET structure as can be seen in Figure 5.7(b). At V_g = 20V, pronounced difference in the current can be observed between the pristine and the adsorbed configuration that resulted in an extreme η ~300% which at V_g = 10V also stays very high at 200%. Within a large V_g range of -20V to +20V, the IV-characteristics in the adsorbed configurations are illustrated in Figure 5.7(c). With an increase in the bias, the difference in the current gets enhanced which is maximum at V_g = 10V, -10V with a maximum $\Delta I \sim 36.5$ μA. At higher values of V_g = 20V, -20V, it is also significantly large at 26μA at 2V bias. Firstly, the presence of such large current ($\sim$ 45μA) at both positive and negative values of V_g confirms the ambipolar nature of the APNR stays intact in the adsorbed configuration. Secondly, the transverse electric field of the gate voltage offers a better enhancement of current in the adsorbed configuration compared to its pristine counterpart. This points towards the impact of presence of Benzene molecule on the conduction behaviour of APNR. The large change in the current due to a change of V_g suggests that a backgate can control the conduction response in a reversible manner without bringing permanent changes in the material.

Apart from the configuration discussed in this work, the conductance modulation was observed irrespective of the adsorption configuration considered from top or side of the nanoribbon. This effect is present under the influence of various external influences like (a) application of strain, (b) presence of dopants of various types at different locations and (c) inclusion of a gate voltage, supporting not only the robustness of this conductivity enhancement, but as well further tuneability obtained through the variation of such parameters suggest the global nature of this claim. Based on the trend observed, it is expected that multiple adsorption of molecules will lead to a much larger change in conductivity in such APNR.

As the width of APNR grows, the changes in conductance could be reduced, however, the effect is expected to smear only for large flakes with micron width range, while for nanoribbons of technological interest having few nm width, it still expects the changes to be significant. Experimentally, nanoribbons of similar dimension in 2D crystals have been grown already using multiple routes [105], in lateral heterostructure [106], vertical stacks [107] and from a liquid precursor [108]. Introduction of nanoscale defects [109, 110]with atomic scale uniformity and long-range order in such 2D structures have been demonstrated. In addition, STM-based lithography techniques [106, 111] have been useful in generating preferred edge structure and detection of attached molecules in a nanoribbon. Strain can be induced by means of a bending apparatus, nanoindentation using an atomic force microscope, or by utilizing flexible substrates. [96]. Single molecular detection has been experimentally observed for graphene [98], Carbon Nanotube [112] where decreasing the channel length led to an increase in the sensitivity upto a critical dimension as considered in the present work. These reports suggest possibilities to create nanoribbons of current interest, especially with STM based local oxidation. Such prospect makes our work as a useful guideline for future experiments.

5.5 CONCLUSION

The present study employed NEGF-DFT calculations to exolore the electronic and transport characteristics of a Phosphorene nanoribbon in close proximity to an organic molecule. Our findings reveal a notable modulation of the conduction response in the system. We determined that in the absence of external stimuli, the adsorption of organic molecule (Benzene) causes a substantial alteration in the conduction behavior while the semiconducting properties of Phosphorene remain relatively constant. The conduction modulation has been characterised by a modulation parameter (η) which has a maximum $\sim$ 150% in this environment. We observed that the behaviour can be further controlled by (i) doping, (ii) applying strain and (iii) gate voltage. Independent of the doping type, location and concentration - a paramount amount of change was observed with a maximum $\eta \sim$ 570% with edge doped Sulphur. On the other hand under the application of strain, a colossal enhancement of current and $\eta \sim$ 1528% was measured under 2% tensile strain. The gate voltage offers a controlled tuning of this effect with a maximum conduction change $\eta \sim$ 300% in non-invasive manner. Due to the larger values of measured currents (20-50μA) and a gate controlled conductivity modulation of almost 400% ($\Delta V_g = 10V$) in the adsorbed configuration, the feasibility of practical studies are significantly high thanks to the advancement of the present day nanotechnological tools. The conductivity modulation will be prevalent for nanoribbons with few nm size as commonly required for the fabrication of a semiconducting channel in a present-day electronic device, compared to that of a much wider nanoribbon with larger numbers of central transport pathways.Our current findings provide new insight about proximity induced tuning and control of the conduction response of Phosphorene and propose new direction for its usefulness in various nanoscale applications in switching, superior sensing and energy efficient designs etc.

6

STRAIN-CONTROLLED OPERATION OF BI_2SE_3 ISLAND SINGLE ELECTRON TRANSISTOR FOR CHEMICAL SENSING AND SWITCHING APPLICATIONS

ABSTRACT

This study presents an investigation into the operation of a Bi_2Se_3 island based single-electron transistor (SET) and its performance under compressive and tensile strain conditions. Using DFT, we analyzed the impact of strain on the electrostatic coupling parameter (α) and the electrostatic polarization contribution parameter (β), both of which have a significant effect on the charge stability diagram (CSD) and normalized differential conductance. Our findings highlight the potential of strain engineering to manipulate the properties of topological insulators in SETs, providing a promising avenue for further research in this area.

6.1 WHAT IS A SINGLE ELECTRON TRANSISTOR?

Today's electronic devices have been miniaturized to a scale where quantum phenomena may become the dominant factor in their operation, leading to a deviation from classical behavior and a change in their properties. However, this does not necessarily have negative consequences for the electronic industry, as these quantum effects can also be harnessed to create new quantum devices. One area where quantum effects are particularly relevant is in nanoscience, where nano-scale devices are designed and fabricated. One such device is the single electron transistor (SET). SET is a three-terminal device like FET, but it uses a

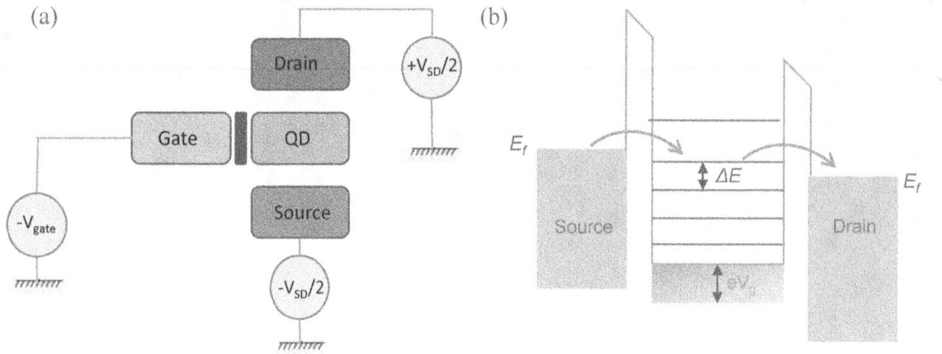

Figure 6.1: (a) Schematic representation of a single-electron transistor, (b) tunnelling of electron from source→island (QD)→drain.

quantum dot or island instead of a channel region. By adjusting the gate bias, we can control the electrostatic potential across the dot, allowing us to add or remove a single electron.

Figure. 6.1(a) illustrates the scematic representation of a SET device. The QD, source, and drain are connected in series via thin insulating barriers that create tunnel junctions. Upon encountering the insulating barrier, the electron is partially transmitted/reflected through it. The total capacitance of the island can be expressed as:

$$C = C_s + C_d + C_g \tag{6.1}$$

Where C_s, C_d and C_g represents the capacitance of source, drain and gate respectively. The conduction of electrons across the insulating barriers in the SET is controlled by the gate. Two primary mechanisms give rise to quantum conduction behavior in a single-electron transistor: (a) Coulomb blockade and (b) sequential electron transport between the source, island, and drain.

The quantum dot or island in the SET contains quantized energy levels. To charge the island with an electron, a specific amount of energy, called the charging energy ($E_c = e^2/2C$), must be applied across the system. If this energy is not provided, electron transport will be blocked. Due to this phenomena, the tunneled electron from the source remains in the island for an extended period, causing a localization effect that erases the previous information carried by the source. This effect ensures that the tunneling of electrons from the island to the drain is independent of the tunneling process from the source to the island.

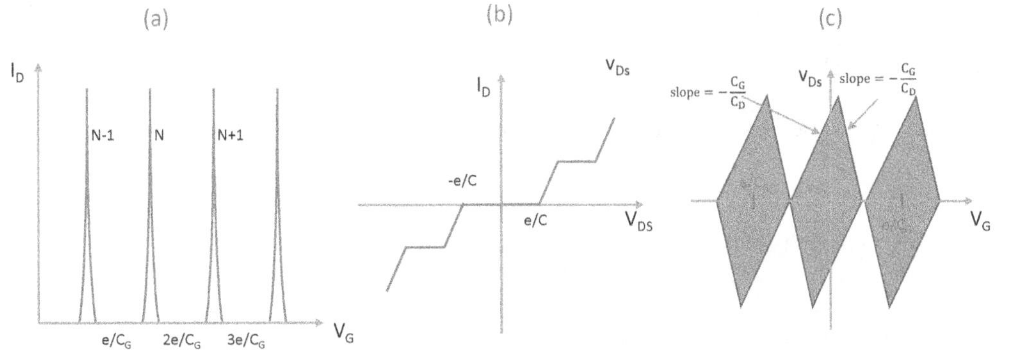

Figure 6.2: (a) I_d-V_g characteristics of the SET at small V_{ds} (b) I_d-V_{ds} characteristics of the SET. (c) The 2D conduction map of V_{ds} and V_g as a function of various value of current.

At $V_{ds} = 0$, the gate voltage can shift the energy level of the island with respect to the Fermi energy (E_f) of the source/drain electrode (Figure 6.1(b)). If the Fermi energy of drain goes above the island and the opposite for drain, this allows the tunnelling of electron through the island. If the Fermi energy of the drain is above that of the island, and vice versa for the source, it enables electron tunnelling through the island, resulting in the SET being in the ON or conducting state. On the other hand when the energy level of source/drain and island are not alligned as previously mentioned for a particular gate bias, the SET device would be in an OFF state. In Figure 6.2(a), the peaks seen in the I_d-V_g plot indicate the inclusion or removal of an electron from the island at a specific gate voltage. The distance between consecutive peaks is represented by:

$$\Delta V_g = \frac{e}{C_g} \tag{6.2}$$

On the other hand, the variation of source-drain bias (V_{ds}) also moves the energy levels, allowing electron tunneling and SET conduction. The resulting $I_d - V_d$ curve exhibits staircase-like characteristics, as illustrated in Figure. 6.2(b). From the graph, we can deduce that $(V_{ds})_{min} \geq \frac{e}{C}$ to initiate electron conduction, while for V $< \frac{e}{C}$, electron conduction is blocked. Coulomb blockade is the term for this phenomenon. Analyzing the $I_d - V_d$ and $I_d - V_g$ characteristics generates a 2D map of conduction called a Coulomb diamond plot or charge stability diagram. The diamond-shaped region corresponds to the Coulomb blockade state, and the capacitance of the source, drain, and gate can be deduced from the slope of the diamond, as shown in Figure 6.2(c). The charging energy (the energy required to change between charge states) is half the height of the central diamond.

6.2 2D MATERIALS IN SINGLE ELECTRON TRANSISTOR

Atomically thin materials exhibit transparency to electric fields due to their low density of states. The Debye screening length, which is the distance over which an electric field can penetrate a material, is reduced with higher carrier density. In contrast to bulk materials, where the electric field is screened at the surface due to the high carrier density (around $10^{22} cm^{-3}$), resulting in a truncated Debye screening length below the Å level, 2D materials exhibit distinct electronic and capacitive properties due to the confinement effect. This effect prevents 2D materials from screening the electric field perpendicular to the surface, since the vertical arrangement of charges is inhibited. Moreover, the low carrier density (around $10^{12} cm^{-3}$) of 2D materials overshoots the Debye screening length, extending up to several nanometers, which contributes to their transparency to the electric field. This behavior has been reported in several studies [113, 114] and is attributed to the unique characteristics of 2D materials. [115, 116]

Now, atomically thin layered topological insulators (2D TI) are a notable addition to the two dimensional layered materials family. Topological insulators a special class of materials that exhibit unique time reversal symmetry-protected helical conducting edge states with an insulating bulk. such states originates because of the spin orbit coupling interaction. Now, devices based on the confinement of topological insulators can be a promising way to study the confined topological states and pave the way for building low energy dissipative logic circuits. The conducting edge-states and the the Klein tunneling makes the confinement of electron in a TI island quite challenging. Till now two groups have demonstrated the single electron transistor and Field effect transistor based on Bi_2Se_3 [117] and Bi_2Te_3 [118] respectively.

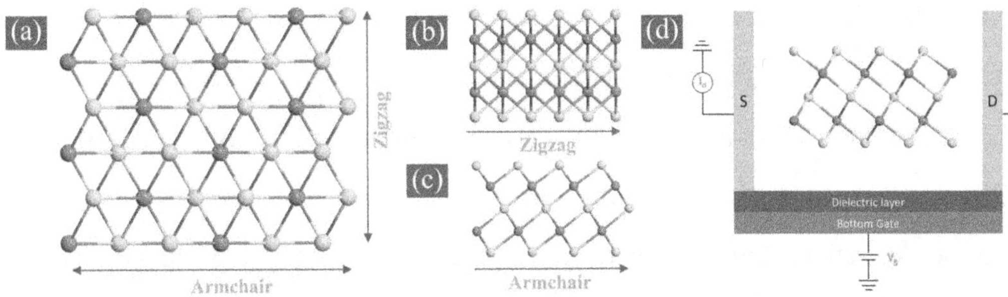

Figure 6.3: (a) Schematics of the (a)top (upper) and (b) and (c) side (lower) views of Bi_2Se_3 monolayer. x- and y-axis are for zigzag and armchair directions where arrow's direction indicated towards the compressive and tensile strain. (d) The schematic representation of a SET device based on Bi_2Se_3 as an island.

This study utilizes First-principles calculations to investigate the behavior and operation of a Bi_2Se_3 island based SET device. Tensile and compressive strains were applied to the Bi_2Se_3 to examine the electrostatic and conduction properties of the SET. Additionally, the impact of adsorbing various toxic gas molecules on SET characteristics, such as charge transfer, charging and binding energy, etc., was investigated. The impact of of strain and the adsorption of gas molecules within the SET was identified using line scans obtained from charge stability diagrams.

6.3 COMPUTATIONAL DETAILS

Quantum Atomistix toolkit software were used to design and investigate the single electron transistor structure. We implemented NEGF-DFT frameowrk [119, 120] to calculate the transport properties of the SET. The study utilized SGGA calculations with the PBE functional, including Van der Waals interactions with the Grimme-D2 approach. Equipotential surfaces of metallic electrodes were used as Neumann's boundary conditions to solve the Poisson's equation. A $9\times9\times1$ Monkhorst pack k-point grid was used. The system was fully relaxed until the force on each atom was less than 10^{-3} eV/Å.

6.4 SYSTEM DESCRIPTIONS

Similar to other 2D materials, Bi_2Se_3 exhibits anisotropic behavior along both the x-axis (zigzag direction) and y-axis (armchair direction) shown in Figure. 6.3.(a)-(c). The Schematic diagram of the SET device where the transport direction is along y-axis (armchair direction) is presented in Figure. 6.3(d). For convenience from now on we would designate the SET device where the transport direction is along along armchair and zigzag direction to be BS_x-SET and BS_y-SET respectively as we later introduced the strain along the transverse direction of the transport direction. Now, to prepare the island for the SET device we first cleaved the Bi_2Se_3 crystal in (001) direction and made a mono-layer. A 2 × 2 supercell of Bi_2Se_3 slab. The strain along x -axis is applied along $x(\epsilon_x)$ and y-axis $y\epsilon_y$) are defined as:

$$\epsilon_x = \frac{(a - a_0)}{a_0}; \epsilon_y = \frac{(b - b_0)}{b_0} \tag{6.3}$$

where $a(a_0)$, $b(b_0)$ are the lattice parameters in the strained(unstrained) configuration along x, y directions. When the transport direction is along the zigzag direction, the outer box of the unstrained system had dimensions of 14.414 Å × 28.64Å × 27.92Å, which included the source, drain, and gate electrodes oriented as follows: 14.414 Å × 28.64Å × 4Å, 14.414 Å × 28.64Å × 4Å, and 14.414Å × 4Å × 28Å. For the SET configuration with the transport direction along the armchair direction of the lattice, the dimensions of the outer box were 16.3344Å × 28.64Å × 26Å, with the source, drain, and gate electrode regions measuring 16.3344Å × 28.64Å × 4Å, 16.3344Å × 28.64Å × 4Å, and 16.3344Å × 4Å × 26Å, respectively. In both configurations, a 4 Å-thick dielectric layer with a dielectric constant of $10\epsilon_0$ (where ϵ_0 is the permittivity of free space) supported the bottom gate electrode. Gold was used as the electrode material for the source, drain, and gate. The dimensions of the outer box and electrodes were adjusted accordingly in the strained configuration.

To invetigate the gas sensing capability of Bi_2Se_3 islands within the SET, six different inorganic molecules were examined: CO, CO_2, NO, NO_2.

Figure. 6.4.(a) and (b) depict the variation of the total energy of the island region of the SET as a function of gate voltage (V_g) for the BS_x-SET and BS_y-SET devices, respectively. The energy (E) of the Bi_2Se_3 slab for different charge states (q) can be expressed as:

$$E(q, V_g) = E_0 + \alpha q V_g + \beta(eV_g)^2 + qW \tag{6.4}$$

Here, E_0 is constant, W denotes the work function of the metallic gold electrode (5.28 eV). The values of α and β are obtained via least-square fitting of Eqn. 6.4 for different charge state (-2, -1, 0, 1, 2) and we averaged them to obtain α_{avg} and β_{avg}. The parameter 'α' indicates the electrostatic coupling between the gate electrode(s) and the island is influenced by the position/orientation of the island with respect to the gate. And 'β' denotes the electrostatic polarization's contribution to the SET structure's overall energy. From the fitting we estimated α_{avg} to be 0.3779 and 0.34857 for BS_x-SET and BS_y-SET respectively. On the other hand, the value of β_{avg} was found to be -0.05571 eV^{-1} and -0.05531 eV^{-1} for BS_x-SET and BS_y-SET respectively. Here. we obsreved for the unstrained configuration α_{avg} is higher than β_{avg} for both BS_x-SET and BS_y-SET indicating that the elctrostatic coupling between the gate and island is higher compared to the electrostatic polarization towards total energy.

Generating a charge stability diagram can provide further insight into the conduction characteristics of the single-electron transistor (SET) in the weak coupling regime. By utilizing sequential tunneling, the conduction behavior of the SET device has to follow:

$$e|V_d|/2 > (E_c + W) > -e|V_d|/2 \tag{6.5}$$

In the V_d-V_g plane, Figure. 6.4(c)-(d) shows the charge stability diagram for both BS_x-SET and BS_y-SET, represented by diamond shapes. Each colored diamond region represents a different charge state of the island, indicating a Coulomb blockade where no transport occurs. The island's charging energy in its ground state is 1.1 eV for BS_x-SET and 1.125 eV for BS_y-SET, as indicated by the height of the central diamond in each diagram. (Figure. 6.2(c))

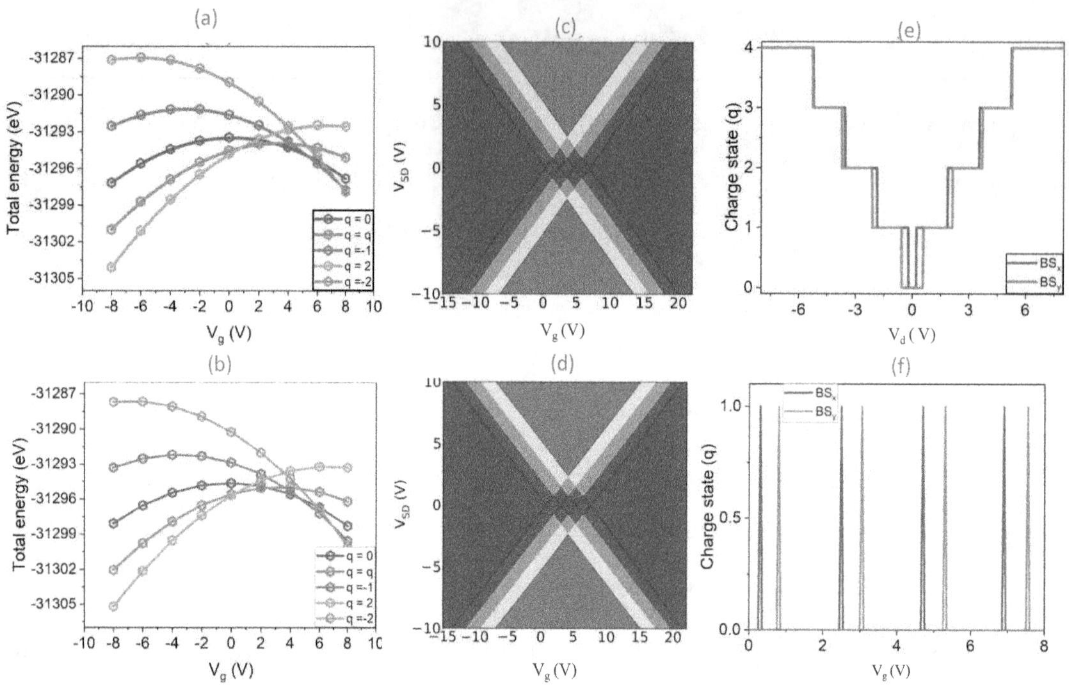

Figure 6.4: (a)The total energy of the alpha-borophene island for different charge state as a function of gate voltage V_g for (a) BS_x and (b) BS_y respectively. The charge stability diagram of the Bi_2Se_3 island for (a) BS_x-SET and BS_y-SET.

The charging energy (E_c), defined as the specific amount of energy greater than the Coulomb blockade energy required for transport to occur, corresponds to a temperature above room temperature. We found both values of E_c to be $\approx 10^4$K for BS_x-SET and BS_y-SET. The voltage necessary for switching between the ON and OFF states of a nanoelectronic device, represented by V_{sw}, is determined by the change in energy level across the central diamond regime. We determined V_{sw} to be 1.64 eV and 1.56 eV for BS_x-SET and BS_y-SET, respectively .

We also analyzed line scans along the horizontal and vertical axis of the Charge stability diagram for different charge states. Figure 6.4(e) and (f) represent the vertical and horizontal line scans, respectively. The step-like features observed along V_d at a constant V_g depend on the charging energy of the island, which varies for different charge states. We observed that BS_y-SET exhibited a wider width compared to BS_x-SET, which is consistent with the calculated value obtained previously. Moreover, the peaks observed in the horizontal line scans taken along V_g at constant V_d represent the addition and removal of electrons from the islands. We observed that the peaks occurred at a higher gate voltage for BS_y-SET compared

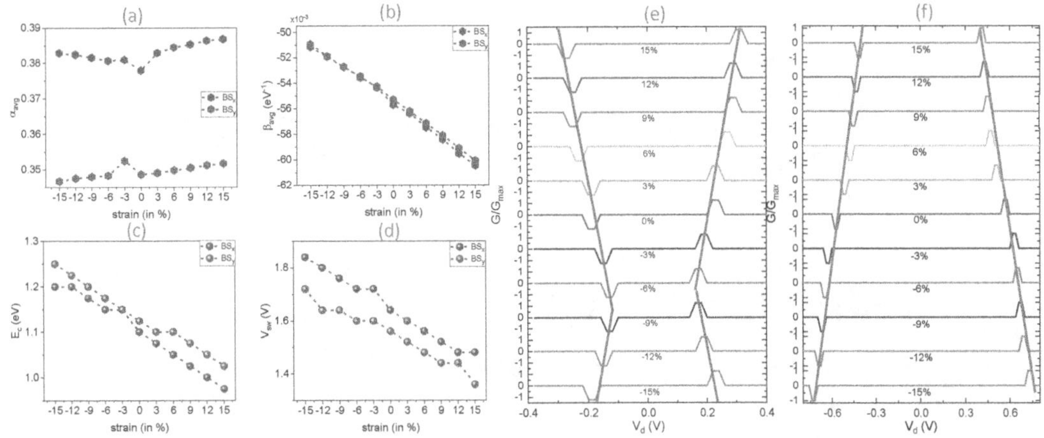

Figure 6.5: Variation of (a) α_{avg}, (b) β_{avg} (c) E_c and (d) V_{sw} of BS_x-SET and BS_y-SET as a function of strain along x-and y-directions respectively. Variation of normalised differential conductance as a function of V_d for (e) BS_x-SET and (f) BS_y-SET device.

to BS_x-SET, and the separation between the peaks was slightly higher for BS_y-SET than for BS_x-SET.

6.5.1 IMPACT OF STRAIN OF ON ELECTROSTATIC AND CONDUCTION BEHAVIOUR

The variations of α_{avg} and β_{avg} with strain for BS_x-SET and BS_y-SET are shown in Figures 6.5(a) and (b), respectively. The strain range examined in this study ranged from -15% to 15%. As shown in these plots, we can observe that with an increase in tensile strain, α_{avg} consistently increased, reaching a maximum value of 0.38679 eV^{-1} for BS_x and 0.35163 eV^{-1} for BS_y at ϵ_x = 15%. Figure 6.5(a) demonstrates that, when subjected to compressive strain, the electrostatic coupling between the gate and the island was stronger in the x-direction compared to the y-direction. In all strained configurations, the magnitude of the quadratic term β_{avg} was noticeably smaller than the linear term α_{avg}. This finding suggests that the gate is the primary factor governing the electrostatic operation of the SET, rather than electrostatic polarization contributions. This is consistent with the planar island structure used in this study. Application of strain to the island resulted in a decrease in the charging energy for both BS_x-SET and BS_y-SET, with a consistent reduction observed as the strain increased. The charging energy ranged from 1-1.6 eV, corresponding to a temperature of 10^4 K, well above room temperature. Notably, the charging energy was substantially lower for BS_x in both tensile and compressive strain regions compared to the BS_y island within the SET.

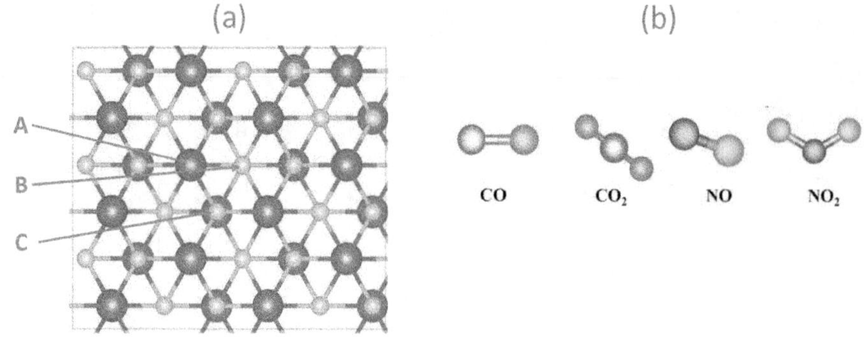

Figure 6.6: Schematic of the (a) positions to be be tested and (b) orientations of different gas molecules: CO, CO_2, NO, NO_2.

The SET's switching performance is defined by the voltage (V_{sw}) required to switch its ON and OFF states, which is determined by the change in the energy level across the central diamond regime. Similar to the charging energy, the switching voltage also monotonically decreased as the strain increased from -15% to 15%. However, the overall value of V_{sw} was higher for the BS_x-SET compared to the BSy-SET. At -15% strain, the highest values of Vsw were observed to be 1.84 eV and 1.72 eV for the BS_x-SET and BS_y-SET, respectively.

6.5.2 IMPACT OF STRAIN ON THE CHARGE STABILITY DIAGRAM (CSD)

To understand the evolution of CSD, a series of line scans were conducted for each strained configuration. The horizontal line scans were performed by fixing the drain voltage (V_d) at 0.05 V and recording the variation of the charge state (q) along the gate voltage (V_g) axis. The resulting data was then used to calculate the normalized differential conductance, as shown in Figure.6.5. The analysis revealed that for strain levels between -15% and 15%, the first order of conduction peaks occurred within the range of 0.14-0.28 V and 0.4-0.72 V for BS_x-SET and BS_y-SET, respectively. These findings suggest that the system is capable of operating at low power. Additionally, it was observed that changing the sign of the voltage across the drain electrode resulted in changes in conductance. For BS_x-SET, the conduction initially shifted towards zero as the strain increased from -15% to -9%, before steadily increasing up to 15% strain. In contrast, for BS_y-SET, a steady shift towards zero was observed as strain levels increased from -15% to 15%.

6.5.3 ADSORPTION OF INORGANIC IDENTITIES DEPENDENT BEHAVIOUR OF THE SET

To expand upon our research how different gas molecules affect the transport behavior of SET. Nearby molecules can affect the island's charge state due to quantized conduction. Our study focused on four common atmospheric molecules: CO, CO_2, NO, and NO_2. We found the most stable positions and orientations for these molecules based on minimum energy.. Three possible locations were considered on the island: above the Bi atom of the Bi_2Se_3 quintuple layer (site A), above the Se atom of the top layer of the Bi_2Se_3 quintuple layer (site B), and above the Se atom of the middle layer of the Bi_2Se_3 quintuple layer (site C), as depicted in Figure. 6.6. We factored in molecule orientation up, down and vertical (u, d, v) to find the optimal adsorption configuration on the monolayer. The binding strength was estimated with the adsorption energy (E_a), calculated by this equation::

$$E_a = E_{layer} + E_{molecule} - E_{layer+molecule} \tag{6.6}$$

We found that NO and CO_2 had negative binding energies in the adsorbed configuration for the Bi_2Se_3 slab, indicating that it is not feasible for these molecules to be adsorbed on the slab. E_{layer} represents the 2D layer energy, $E_{molecule}$ represents the molecule energy, and $E_{layer+molecule}$ is the equilibrium energy of the combined layer and molecule system within the SET. Therefore, we proceeded to perform SET calculations only for CO and NO_2. We found no notable change in the values of α_{avg} and β_{avg} with the unadsorbed configuration.

In Figure 6.7(a), the charging energy (E_c) of the island reflects the impact of adsorption of gas molecules. Our observations indicate that for BS_x-SET, the adsorption of CO and NO_2 caused a slight increase in E_c. For BS_y-SET, CO adsorption also led to a slight increase in E_c, but there was no change for NO_2 adsorption. In terms of switching voltage, there was no change in either BS_x-SET or BS_y-SET upon NO_2 adsorption. However, V_{sw} decreased for BS_x-SET and increased for BS_y-SET. For BS_x-SET, there was no change in the first conduction peak after NO_2 adsorption, but for CO adsorption, the peak slightly shifted

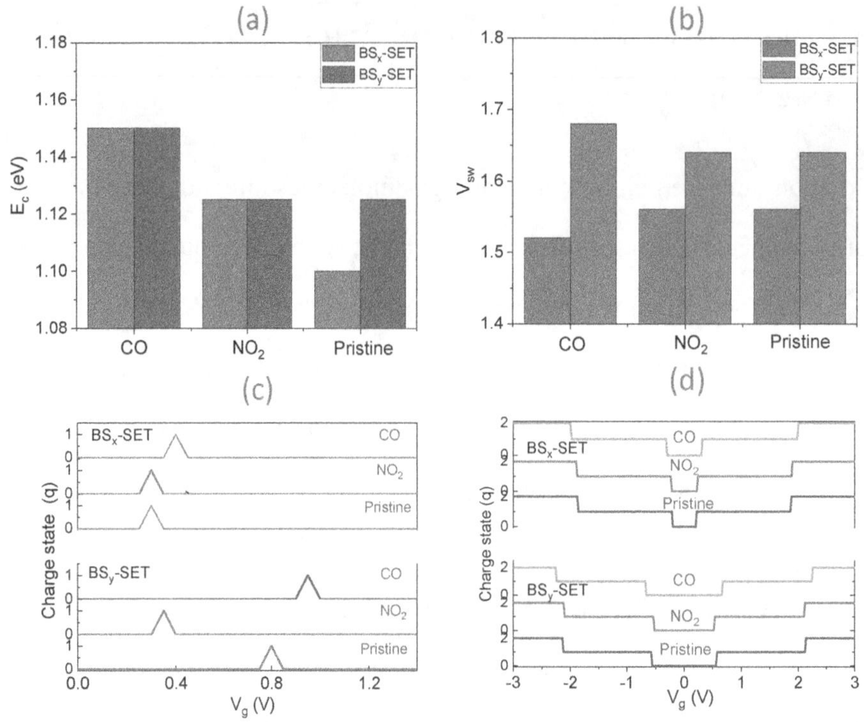

Figure 6.7: The variation of (a) Charging energy (E_c), (b) switching voltage (V_{sw}), (c) V_g at constant V_d from the charge stability diagram for both BS$_x$-SET and BS$_y$-SET and (d) normalised differential conductance as a function of V_d for BS$_x$-SET and BS$_y$-SET.

towards zero. In contrast, for BS$_y$-SET, there was no change in the first conduction peak, but after CO adsorption, the peak shifted towards a higher value. After the adsorption of NO_2, there was no change in the width of the horizontal line scan for both BS$_x$-SET and BS$_y$-SET. However, the width increased after CO adsorption.

6.6 CONCLUSION

In this study, first we investigated the impact of strain on the operation and charging energy of BS$_x$-SET and BS$_y$-SET. We found that tensile strain consistently increases αavg. On the one hand, when we increase the overall value of compressive strain, increasing trend is obesreved α_{avg} for BS$_x$-SET and the opposite for BS$_y$-SET. Line scans were performed, and changing the voltage across the drain electrode resulted in different conductance trends for the two types of SETs. In a separate study on gas molecule adsorption, CO slightly increased the charging energy for both devices, while NO_2 had no effect on BS$_y$-SET and slightly increased the charging energy of BS$_x$-SET. The switching voltage was affected differently for both devices upon the adsorption of CO and NO_2, and the first conduction peak and the width of the horizontal line scan were also impacted differently depending on the molecule and device.

7

TEMPERATURE AND FREQUENCY-DEPENDENT RESISTIVE SWITCHING PROPERTIES OF COPPER IODIDE AND $LA_{0.7}SR_{0.3}MNO_3$ BASED COMPOSITE SYSTEMS UNDER VARIOUS DC AND AC EXCITATIONS

ABSTRACT

In this chapter, we studied the impact of temperature and frequency on the resistive switching (RS) behavior of (1-x)CuI.(x)$La_{0.7}Sr_{0.3}MnO_3$ nanocomposites with x values ranging from 0.001 to 0.05. We chose copper iodide for its wide direct bandgap (3.1 eV), high exciton binding energy, electrosensitivity, high hole mobility, and photosensitivity [121, 122]. $La_{0.7}Sr_{0.3}MnO_3$ was chosen for its well-known properties, such as half-metallicity and ferromagnetism even at room temperature [123, 124].

The chapter's first part discusses the temperature-dependent DC resistive switching behavior of the nanocomposites from 150K to 300K. Analysis of current versus voltage plots at room temperature shows Schottky emission and Poole-Frenkel effect as the dominant transport mechanisms in the low and high bias regions, respectively. Addition of $La_{0.7}Sr_{0.3}MnO_3$ enhances the RS response, confirmed by X-ray photoemission spectroscopy (XPS). Endurance tests reveal the highest ON/OFF ratios averaged over 100 cycles to be 4.2 ± 1.14 and 3.8 ± 0.35 for x=0.001 and 0.02, respectively, at 300K. The optimal ON/OFF ratios at 250K are 19.8 ± 1.85 for x=0.001 and 22.7 ± 4.17 for x=0.02.

The chapter's second part focuses on pulse-induced resistance switching behavior in the nanocomposite system. Hysteretic pulse current-voltage measurements reveal Schottky emission and Poole-Frenkel effect as the dominant mechanisms in the lower and higher bias regions, respectively. The resistive switching behavior is stable over 1000 cycles of square electrical pulse train measurements using frequencies of 125 Hz and 250 Hz.

7.1 INTRODUCTION

Memory and processing technology have made great strides in speed and power efficiency over the last few decades, but current memory devices have hit the scaling limits predicted by Moore's law and suffer from drawbacks such as heat issues, high costs for manufacturing ultra-large-scale projects, and susceptibility to device strain. This has led scientists to a venture for building alternative memory devices/architectures that can satisfy the ever-increasing need for more powerful processing power in digital/analog electronics, neural networks, data storage, artificial intelligence, etc [125]. Therefore, it has become necessary to fabricate a 'universal memory' that can operate at high speed with density circuitry and possess non-volatile storage capacity, thus incorporating the merits of different popular memory devices into a single one. Therefore, the emergence of new NVM (non-volatile memory devices) like phase-change random access memory (PCRAM) [126], spin-transfer torque magnetic RAM (STT-MRAM) [127], ferroelectric RAM (FRAM) [128], resistive RAM (RRAM or ReRAM) and conducting bridge RAM (CBRAM) [129] is gaining huge momentum worldwide. Among the members of the NVM memory family, resistive switching-based memory has attracted huge attention owing to its comparatively easy fabrication process and proven compatibility with complementary metal-oxide semiconductor (CMOS) technology [130], competence for high-density packing of chips through cross-point structure [131], superior performance like high switching speed ($<$10 ns) [132], scalability ($<$ 10nm) [133] and low-power consumption (1pJ/bit) [134], low operational voltage, etc.

Resistive switching has been widely investigated in various kinds of materials like binary oxide [135, 136], transition metal oxide[137, 138], organic materials [139], hybrid/composites, [140] etc. Generally, in oxide-based resistive switching (RS) mediums, the oxygen vacancy plays a crucial role in inducing the high/low resistance states. Now, most oxide-based resistive random access memory (RRAM) requires high-temperature processing for device fabrication. An alternative approach for the low-cost fabrication of RRAM is to use hybrid materials/composites. Resistive switching behavior can be easily introduced in hybrid materials/composites as we can make sufficient charge-trapping defects and interfaces. Various groups have fabricated RS devices by dispersed inorganic materials (metal/oxide nanoparticles) in polymer/organic matrix. Now, this can be a promising way to enhance the RRAM-based performance without compromising the physical properties.

In the first section we addressed the DC response on (1-x)CuI. (x)LSMO nanocomposites by assessing the hysteretic transport measurement.

The study presented in section. 7.3.3 focuses on the resistive switching induced by pulsed voltage in nanocomposites. The study explores the influence of various parameters, such as pulse width, delay time, duty cycle, and more, on the ON/OFF ratio of the nanocomposite system. All the measurements of section. 7.3.3 were conducted at room temperature using hysteretic pulsed I-V and square electrical pulse train I-V measurements.

7.2 EXPERIMENTAL DETAILS

We procured copper iodide (CuI) along with the precursor chemicals (La_2O_3, $SrCO_3$, and Mn_2O_3) for synthesizing $La_{0.7}Sr_{0.3}MnO_3$ (LSMO) from Sigma-Aldrich, all of which possess a minimum purity of 99.99%. To synthesize $La_{0.7}Sr_{0.3}MnO_3$, we grinded stoichiometric amounts of La_2O_3, $SrCO_3$, and Mn_2O_3 in acetone for 5 hours, calcined the mixture at 1200°C for 12 hours with a heating/cooling rate of approximately 3°C/min, and ground the resulting powder for 1 hour to ensure homogeneity.

For structural characterization of CuI, $La_{0.7}Sr_{0.3}MnO_3$ and their nanocomposites, we performed XRD, TEM, XPS. XRD was conducted with a scan rate of 2^0 per min and a step size of 0.02°. To perform TEM and XPS measurement, the powder is collected from the region between the two electrodes of the device following the termination of the SET process, exactly after switching the device from a high resistance state (HRS) to a low resistance state (LRS).

For transport measurement, the powder of nanocomposite samples was consolidated into pellets of 6 mm diameter and 2 mm thickness. After that, we carefully applied the silver paste on top of the pellets, which will act as electrodes, and maintained a distance of 1mm between them. Next, we put the pellets inside a micro-manipulated vacuum probe system. Entire transport measurements were conducted in a vacuum environment using a two-probe approach with a Keithley 2634B sourcemeter and the base pressure was kept at 2×10^{-4} mbar at room temperature. Next, two probes made of tungsten were stationed on top of the silver dots to complete the connection to the Keithley sourcemeter. Compliance current was set to be 100 mA throughout the measurement to evade any likelihood of permanent dielectric breakdown and leakage current contribution to the sample.

7.3 RESULT AND DISCUSSION

7.3.1 STRUCTURAL CHARACTERIZATION

We have used Fullprof™ software to perform Rietveld refinement of the XRD plot of CuI, $La_{0.7}Sr_{0.3}MnO_3$ and (1-x) CuI.(x) LSMO composites. CuI and $La_{0.7}Sr_{0.3}MnO_3$ belongs to $R\bar{3}c$ and $F\bar{4}3m$ space group respectively. The XRD plots of pristine copper iodide and $La_{0.7}Sr_{0.3}MnO_3$ (LSMO) are shown in Figure. 7.1(a), (b) respectively. The statistical refinement parameters for $La_{0.7}Sr_{0.3}$ MnO_3 were R_p = 15.3, R_{wp} = 23.7, R_{exp} = 3.63 and χ^2 = 3.01.

We adopted two-phase Rietveld refinement for (1-x)CuI.(x)LSMO with x= 0.001, 0.005, 0.01, 0.02, and 0.05 nanocomposites. The refinement parameter χ^2: 2.36, 2.17, 2.47, 2.31 for x = 0.005, 0.01, 0.02, and 0.05, respectively, imply a good fitting with the observed and calculated data. From the output file, the volume and weight ratio between the two-phase, i.e., CuI and LSMO, can be deduced. From the multiphase Rietveld refinement, we inferred the

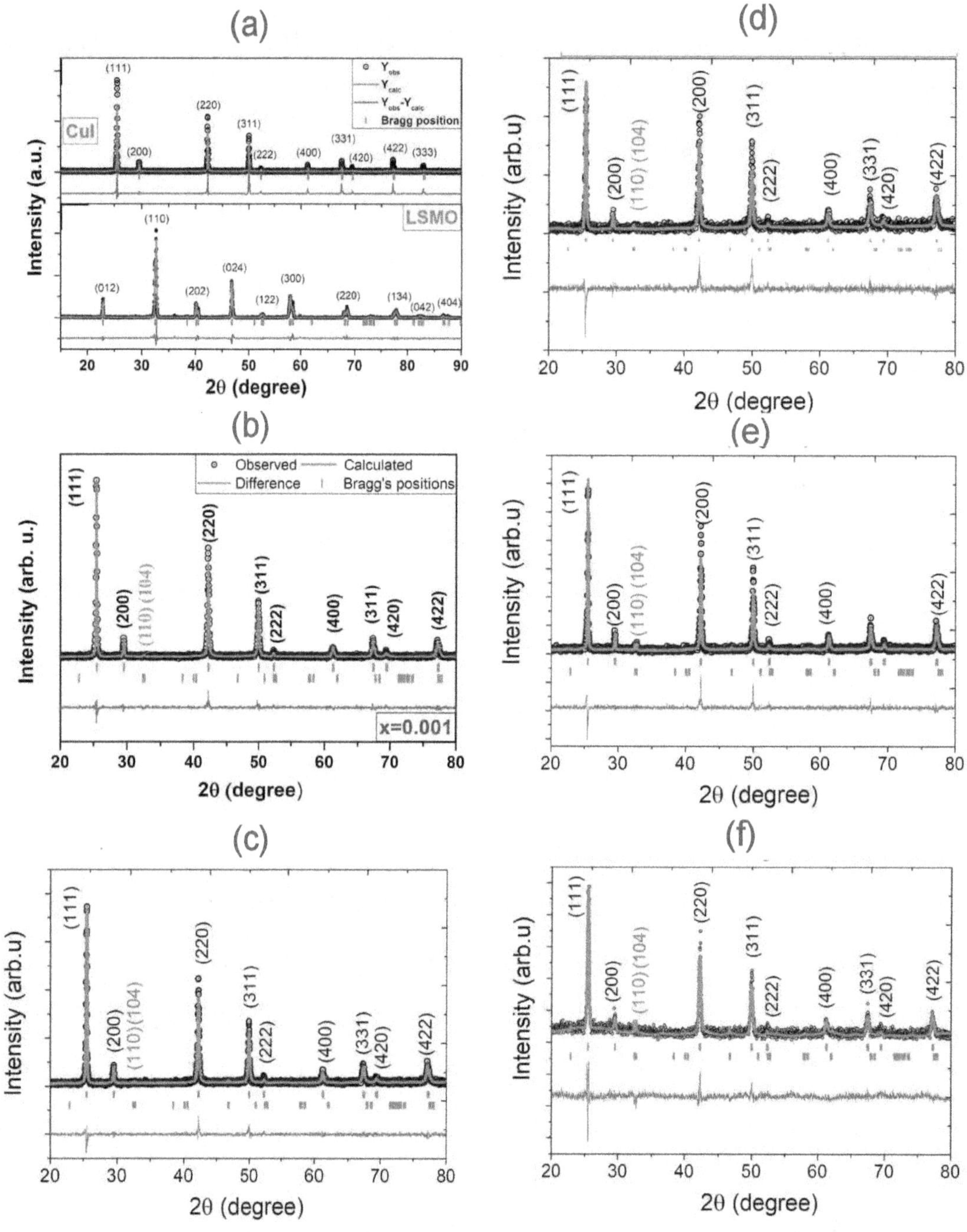

Figure 7.1: Rietveld refinement pattern for (a) CuI and (b) $La_{0.7}Sr_{0.3}MnO_3$ (LSMO). Two-phase Rietveld refinement pattern for (1-x)CuI.(x)LSMO nanocomposite with (b) x=0.001, (c) x=0.005, (d) x= 0.01 and (e) x=0.02 and (f) x = 0.05.The experimentally observed, computed, and differences between curves are labeled, along with Bragg's position and Miller indices. Bragg's positions and the corresponding Miller indices for $La_{0.7}Sr_{0.3}MnO_3$ is shown are highlighted in green color.

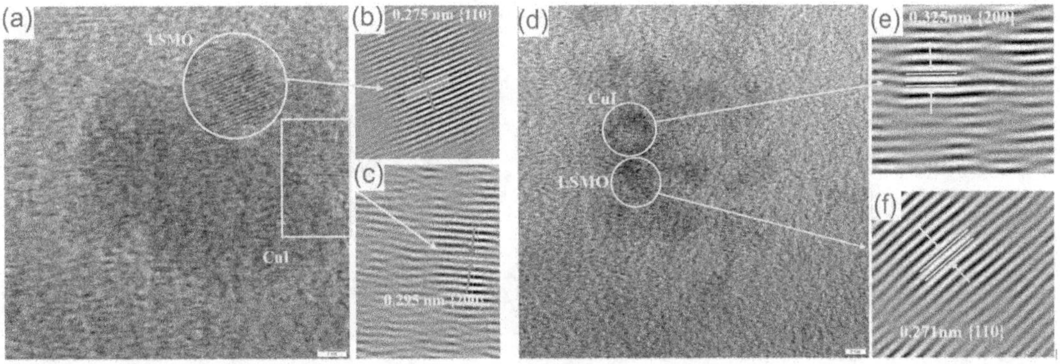

Figure 7.2: (a) HRTEM micrograph of nanocomposite with x=0.001. (b), (c) denotes the 'd' spacing associated with CuI and LSMO, respectively.(d) HRTEM image of nanocomposite with x=0.02. (e), (f) denotes the 'd' spacing associated with LSMO and CuI, respectively.

actual value of 'x' to be 0.22%, 0.83%, 1.27%, 2.12%, and 5.59% for x = 0.001, 0.005, 0.01, 0.02, and 0.05 respectively.

To analyze the sample's local composition, we performed HRTEM measurements. In Figure. 7.2(d) we presented the HRTEM images of the nanocomposite with x= 0.02. To determine the lattice parameter from the HRTEM images, we performed Fast Fourier Transform (FFT) of the selected area as shown in Figure. 7.2(e) and Figure. 7.2(e). Here, we observed two distinct inter-planar distance spacing; 0.275 nm (in Figure. 7.2(e)) and 0.295 nm (in Figure. 7.2(f)). Now, the 'd' spacing 0.295 nm is associated with the peak of copper iodide (2θ = 29.26^0) having a plane of {200}. On the other hand, the 'd' spacing 0.275 nm is associated with the peak of $La_{0.7}Sr_{0.3}MnO_3$ $2\theta = 32.49^0$ having a plane of {110}. This confirms the presence of $La_{0.7}Sr_{0.3}MnO_3$ and CuI in the nanocomposite.

7.3.2 TRANSPORT STUDY

7.3.2.1 DC RESISTIVE SWITCHING BEHAVIOR IN (1-X)CUI. (X) LSMO COMPOSITE SAMPLES AT ROOM TEMPERATURE

We performed the current-voltage measurement at room temperature by applying voltage in 0V→4V→-4V→0V order, where the sweep rate was set to be 0.5 V/s. Then, we repeated the hysteretic I-V measurement for 100 successive cycles for all the nanocomposites.

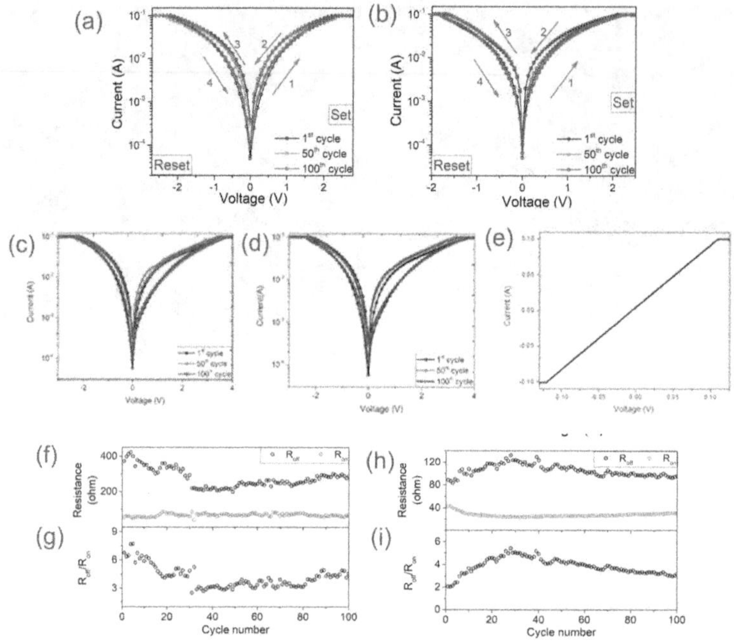

Figure 7.3: (a) Hysteretic I-V plots of 1st, 50th and 100th cycle for (a) x=0.001 and (b) x=0.02, (c) x=0.005. (d) x = 0.01. (e) represents the 1st Hysteretic I-V cycle for x = 0.05. (f) and (g) represents the R_{ON}, R_{OFF} value and corresponding ON/OFF ratio for each consecutive cycle for 100th cycles for x=0.001 at T=300 K. (h) and (i) represents similar plots for x= 0.02 at T=300 K.

The hysteretic I-V plot for different cycles and compositions were presented in Figure. 7.3(a)-(d). The device underwent a 'Set' procedure from high to low resistance in positive polarity and a 'Reset' operation from low to high resistance in negative polarity. The nanocomposite exhibited stable I-V plots over 100 cycles. Similar resistive switching behavior was observed for x= 0.005 and 0.01. However, the nanocomposite with x=0.05 had a linear current-voltage relation, and no hysteresis was observed.

To further investigate the robustness of the resistive switching behavior, we examined the ON/OFF ratio derived from the I-V curves recorded during RS cycling through a DC voltage sweep. Figure. 7.3(c) and Figure. 7.3(d) represent the R_{OFF}, R_{ON} value and corresponding ON/OFF ratio for x=0.001 for 100 cycles. Similar plots for x= 0.02 are presented in Figure. 7.3(e) and Figure. 7.3(f). Additionally, we also calculated the statistical distribution variables like mean and standard deviation of the ON/OFF ratio using the following formulas

$$mean = \mu = \tilde{x} = \frac{\sum x}{n} \tag{7.1}$$

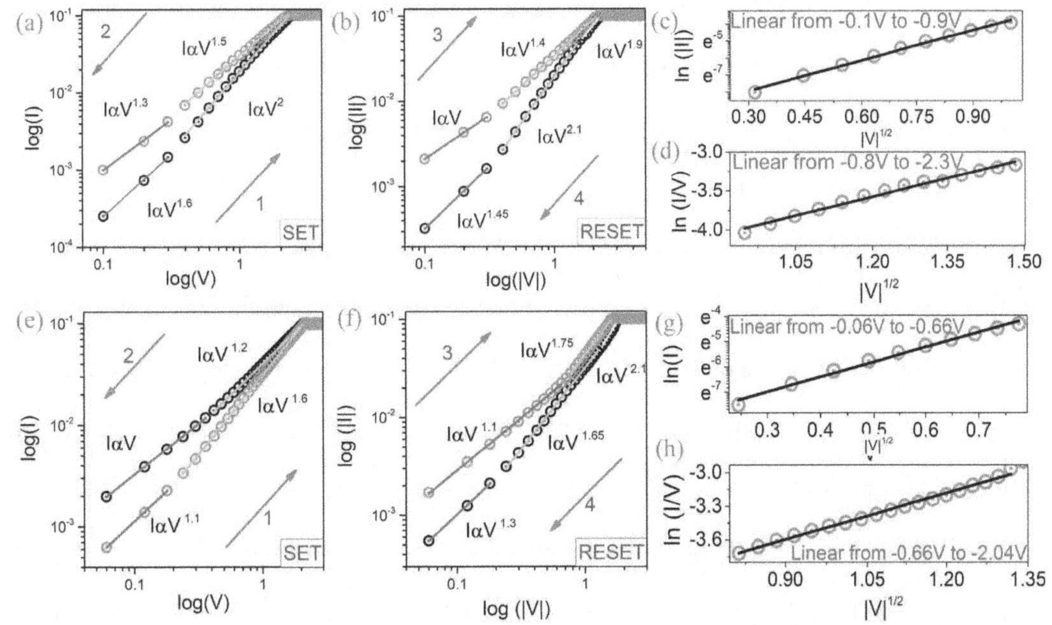

Figure 7.4: (a) log-log I-V plot of positive polarity ('SET' process) and (b) log-log |I|-|V| plot of negative polarity ('RESET' process) for x= 0.001. Linear fitting of (c) $\ln(|I|)$-$\sqrt{|V|}$ for Schottky Emission (SE) and (d) $\ln(|I/V|)$-$\sqrt{|V|}$ for Poole-Frenkel (P-F) effect (path '4' in Figure. 7.3(h)) for x=0.001. (e)-(f) analogous to (a)-(d) for x= 0.02.

where 'x' is the ON/OFF ratio value of a particular hysteresis cycle, where 'n' indicates total hysteresis cycles '$\tilde{x}$' is the average ON/OFF ratio value over 'n' cycle, for this experiment, 'n' = 100. and standard deviation

$$SD = \sigma = \sqrt{\frac{\sum(x-\tilde{x})^2}{n-1}} \tag{7.2}$$

The average ON/OFF ratio over 100 cycles was 4.2 ± 1.14 and 3.8 ± 0.35 for x=0.001 and 0.02, respectively.

7.3.2.2 CHARGE TRANSPORT PROPERTIES AND SWITCHING MECHANISMS

In Figure. 7.4(a) and 7.4(b) we have presented the log-log I-V plot for both the 'Set' and 'Reset' processes for x=0.001. The high resistance state (HRS) of the 'Set' process (path '1' in Figure. 7.4(a)) can be divided into two regions with (i) nonlinear behavior ($I \propto V^{1.6}$) at low bias region and (ii) Child's square law, ($I \propto V^2$) at higher bias region. Now, the HRS of the 'Reset' process (path '4' in Figure. 7.4(b)) can also be segmented into two nonlinear regions, (i) I$\propto$ $V^{1.5}$, (ii) I$\propto V^2$ i.e. Child's square law. On the other hand, for x= 0.02 (see Figure. 7.4(e)), the HRS of the 'Set' process can be divided into two regions exhibiting. (i) linear behavior (I$\propto V^{1.2}$) at low voltage region, (ii) nonlinear behavior (I$\propto V^{1.6}$) at higher voltage region. Now, the HRS of the 'Reset' process (see Figure. 7.4(f)) can be categorized into three regions (i) low bias regime where I$\propto V^{1.3}$ (which can be approximated to V) i.e., Ohmic conduction mechanism, (ii) nonlinear region where I$\propto V^{1.7}$ and (iii) increment in the current where I$\propto V^{2.1}$; these can be approximated to Child's square law($\approx V^2$). Now, the log-log I-V plot analysis indicated the possibility of two separate charge transport mechanisms being dominant in different segments of the nonlinear region. Therefore, we matched the I-V plot with the current-voltage relationship associated with various conduction methods.

Next, we fitted the I-V data of the HRS region (see path '4' of Figure. 7.4(b)) of the negative polarity with (a) $\ln(|I|)$ vs. $\sqrt{|V|}$ and (b) $\ln|(I/V)|$ vs. $\sqrt{|V|}$. From the linear fitting, we got (i) Schottky emission (SE) to be dominant in -0.1 V to -0.9 V region (confirmed by the linear fitting of ln(I) vs. $\sqrt{|V|}$ plot in Figure. 7.4(c)) and (ii) Poole-Frenkel (P-F) effect was dominant in -0.8 V to -2.3 V for x=0.001 (see Figure. 7.4(d)). On the other hand, for x= 0.02: (i) Schottky emission (SE) was dominant from -0.06 V to -0.66V and (ii) Poole-Frenkel (P-F) effect was dominant from -0.66 V to -2.04 V supported by the linear fitting of the corresponding region (see Figure. 7.4(g) and Figure. 7.4(h)). Therefore, Schottky emission (which follows $\ln(|I|)$ vs. $\sqrt{|V|}$ relation) and Poole-Frenkel effect (which follows $\ln|(I/V)|$ vs. $\sqrt{|V|}$ relation) turned out to be the main driving charge transport mechanisms in lower and higher bias regions respectively.

Schottky emission is a conduction mechanism that occurs when an electric field induces thermionic emission of electrons across a reduced work-function barrier at the interface of two materials. In oxide-based resistive switching media, the migration of oxygen via oxygen vacancies in a direction-dependent manner causes the creation of an oxygen-deficient or oxygen-rich region at the electrode-switching medium interface, resulting in a change in resistance state. Poole-Frenkel emission is a form of bulk-limited conduction that happens when a moderate electric field is present. It involves trapped electrons being thermally excited into the conduction band with the help of the electric field, and the trapping centers are defects

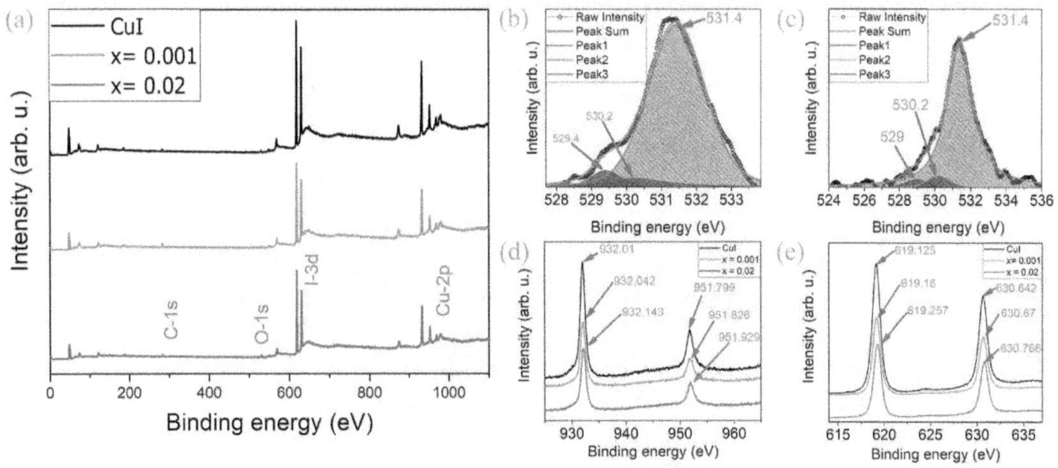

Figure 7.5: (a) Wide scan XPS spectra of pristine copper iodide, nanocomposite with (b) x=0.001 and (c) x=0.02. Short scan range of Oxygen (O) along with fitted XPS curve for (b) x=0.001 and (c) x=0.02. Chemical shift of (d) Cu-2$p_{3/2}$ and Cu-2$p_{1/2}$ as well as (e) I-3$d_{5/2}$ and (e) I-3$d_{3/2}$ with varying concentration of LSMO in the nanocomposites.

in the dielectric material. Based on this conduction mechanism, we hypothesize that copper iodide acted as the dielectric medium, while LSMO served as defect traps by providing oxygen vacancies. Our theory is supported by the analysis of the data of X-ray Photoelectron Spectroscopy (XPS) measurements.

XPS was utilized to elucidate the involvement of oxygen vacancies in resistive switching. In Figure. 7.5(a) we presented the high-resolution XPS spectra for pristine CuI, nanocomposite with x= 0.001 and 0.02 consisting of O-1s, I-3d and, Cu-2p peaks. The C-1s peak (284.6 eV) calibrated the XPS curves. The short-range scan of the O-1S peak was presented for x=0.001 and 0.02 in Figures 7.5(b) and 7.5(c), respectively. As we calculated the area under the peaks for CuI, x= 0.001 and 0.02, we observed that the area under O-1s peak for x = 0.001 and x = 0.02 were significantly higher than pristine copper iodide. Upon fitting the source data using the multi-peaks model with Shirley's background, we deconvoluted the O-1S broad peak into three distinct peaks at binding energies of 529.4 eV, 530.2 eV, and 531.4 eV, respectively. Furthermore, at x = 0.02, the triplet peaks were associated with binding energies of 529.0 eV, 530.2 eV, and 531.4 eV, respectively. Generally, O-1s spectra of LSMO exhibits asymmetric broadband with two or three peaks. The peak in the 528-530 eV region corresponds to the Mn-related lattice oxygen (O^{2-}), whereas in 530-534 eV region the peaks manifest from the

Table 7.1: Ratio of areas of Cu-2$p_{3/2}$ and Cu-2$p_{1/2}$ for CuI, nanocomposite with x= 0.001 and 0.02.

Strain	The area under the peak of Cu-2$p_{3/2}$	The area under the peak of Cu-2$p_{1/2}$	Ratio of area
CuI	33841.150	16871.800	2.00
x = 0.001	18885.790	10065.150	1.88
x = 0.02	17657.540	9677.894	1.82

under-coordinated oxygen at the interface oxygen bonding with La/Sr at A sites in ABO_3 perovskite structure and/or oxygen vacancies i.e. to the oxygen-related defects [141, 142]. Additionally, we also observed in the O-1s peak for x = 0.02 has (i) a sharper intensity peak at 530.2 eV compared to x = 0.001, which is typically associated with the oxygen vacancy, (ii) a larger area under the curve compared to x = 0.001 and (iii) shifted the position of the peak corresponding to Mn-O.

In Figure. 7.5(d) and (e), the peak shift of Cu-2p and I-3d towards higher binding energy as the concentration of LSMO increases is shown. Now, we know that if we modify a specimen by adding electro-negative (compared to the base element) elements or impurities, electron density around the base element will decrease, increasing the binding energy. Therefore, we will observe a shift in the positive direction in binding energy [143]. As the LSMO concentration increased in our study, a positive shift in the peak position in Cu-2p was observed. We have also calculated the ratio of area under the Cu-2$p_{3/2}$ and Cu-2$p_{1/2}$ peaks for CuI, x = 0.001 and 0.02, which can be found in Table. 7.1.

The ratio of area under the Cu-2$p_{3/2}$ and Cu-2$p_{1/2}$ peaks for pristine copper iodide was 2.00, as predicted from a sample with no impurities.. As we increased the concentration of LSMO in copper iodide the ratio between areas decreased gradually. This consolidates our previous claim regarding the role of LSMO (oxygen present in LSMO to be precise) being responsible for the chemical shift in Cu-2p peaks. In summary, we attribute the cause of resistive switching to a high concentration of oxygen in the sample, resulting from oxygen

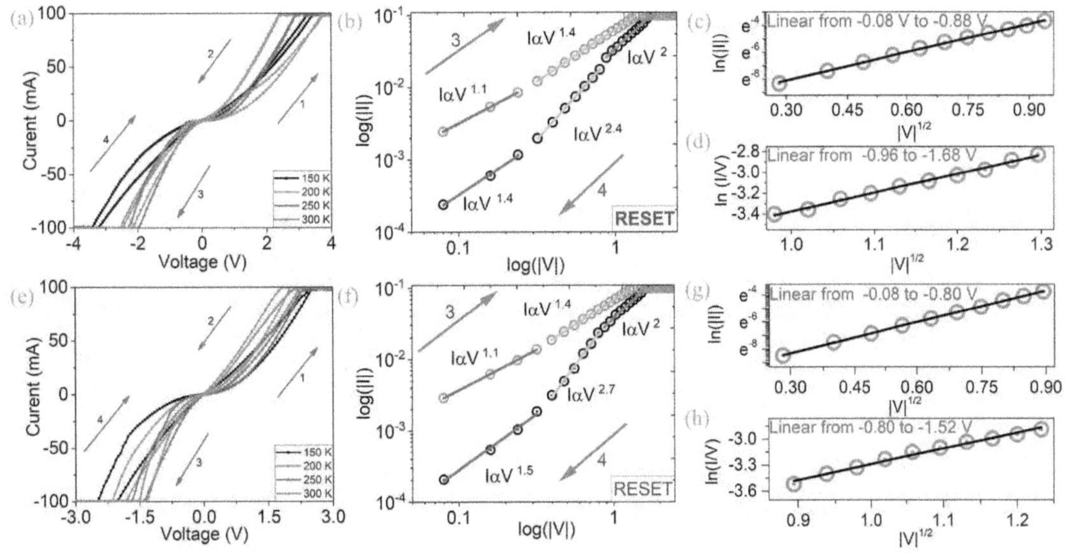

Figure 7.6: (a) Hysteretic I-V curve for x=0.001 temperature T= 150K, 200K, 250K, 300K. (b) log-log I-V of negative polarity for x= 0.001 at T= 250K. (c) ln($|I|$)-$\sqrt{|V|}$ for SE (or negative polarity) and (d) ln($|I/V|$)-$\sqrt{|V|}$ for P-F. (or negative polarity) for x=0.001 at T= 250K. (e)-(h) are analogous to (a)-(d) for x = 0.02.

migration from the surrounding area. This led to a decrease in oxygen concentration and an increase in oxygen vacancy at the interface between the nanocomposite and the electrode. As we discussed earlier, the presence of oxygen vacancy lowers the barrier height of the Schottky barrier, which in turn helped to induce LRS. So, essentially, the system went from 'HRS' to 'LRS'.

Now, for XPS, TEM, we have used the sample taken from the intermediate area of the pellet after the 'SET' process. We did not observe a trace of silver in XPS spectra or HRTEM image. So, this essentially omits the possibility of the migration of silver ions as a potential reason for the emergence of resistive switching in the system.

7.3.3 TEMPERATURE DEPENDENCE OF THE RESISTIVE SWITCHING BEHAVIOR

To understand the impact of temperature on the conduction mechanisms and ON/OFF ratio of the nanocomposites, we have repeated the hysteretic I-V measurement at different temperatures. The hysteretic I-V plots corresponding to the nanocomposites with x= 0.001 and 0.02 at T= 150K, 200K, 250K, and 300K are presented in Figure. 7.6(a), Figure. 7.6(b) respectively. The area between the hysteretic I-V plots also increased as we lowered the temperature. To

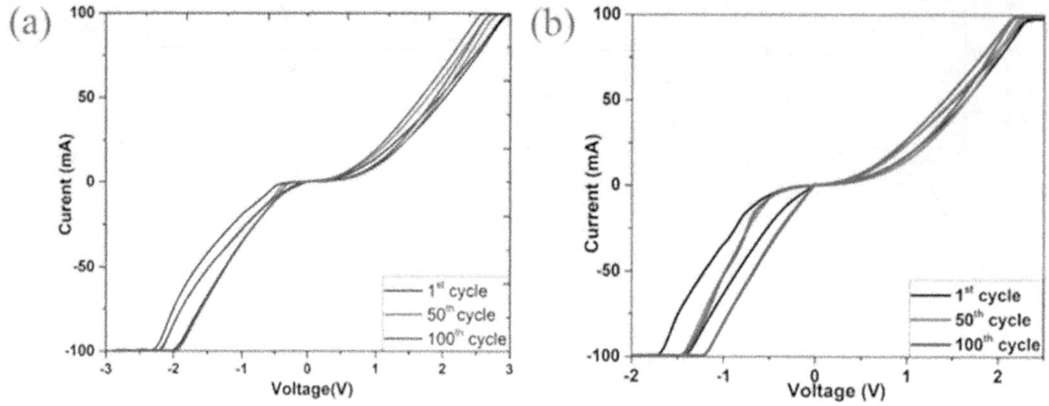

Figure 7.7: Hysteretic I-V plots of 1st, 50th and 100th cycle for (a) x=0.001 and (b) x=0.02 at T = 250 K.

analyze the conduction mechanism, we have plotted log -log I-V of the 'Reset' process for both x= 0.001 (see Figure. 7.6(b)) and x = 0.02 (see Figure. 7.6(f)). Now, the HRS of the 'Reset' process can be divided into three different regions (i) nonlinear behavior ($I \propto V^{1.4}$ for x=0.001 and $I \propto V^{1.5}$ x=0.02) at lower voltage region (ii) steep increase in the slope ($I \propto V^{2.4}$ for x=0.001 and $I \propto V^{2.7}$ x=0.02) and lastly (iii) Child's square law ($I \propto V^2$) for both x=0.001 and x=0.02. From the fitting of the $\ln(|I|)$ vs $\sqrt{|V|}$ and ln(I/V) vs. $\sqrt{|V|}$ curve, we got (i) Schottky emission was dominant in -0.08 V to -0.88 V region for x=0.001 (see Figure. 7.6(c)) and from -0.08 V to -0.80V for x=0.02 (see Figure. 7.6(g)); for higher bias region (ii) Poole-Frenkel effect was dominant from -0.96 V to -1.68 V (see Figure. 7.6(d)) for x=0.001 and from -0.80 V to -1.52 V for x=0.02 (see Figure. 7.6(h). We did a similar analysis for x=0.001 and x=0.02 at T = 200K and 150K. In all the cases, the HRS of the 'Reset' process was dictated by Schottky emission at the lower bias region and Poole-Frenkel emission at the higher bias region.

We also performed endurance test for x = 0.001 and 0.02 sample. Figure 7.7 shows the plots for the 1st, 50th, and 100th cycles of both samples. We have noticed that there is a slight difference in the deviation of the I-V pattern path between the 1st and 50th cycle, as well as the 50th and 100th cycle for both x=0.001 and x=0.02. R_{off} , R_{on} value and their ratio at T= 250K are presented in Figure. 7.8.(a) for x=0.001 and Figure. 7.8.(c) for x=0.02 respectively. The average ON/OFF ratio was 19.8 $\pm$ 1.849 for x=0.001 and 22.7 $\pm$ 4.167 for x=0.02. Now,

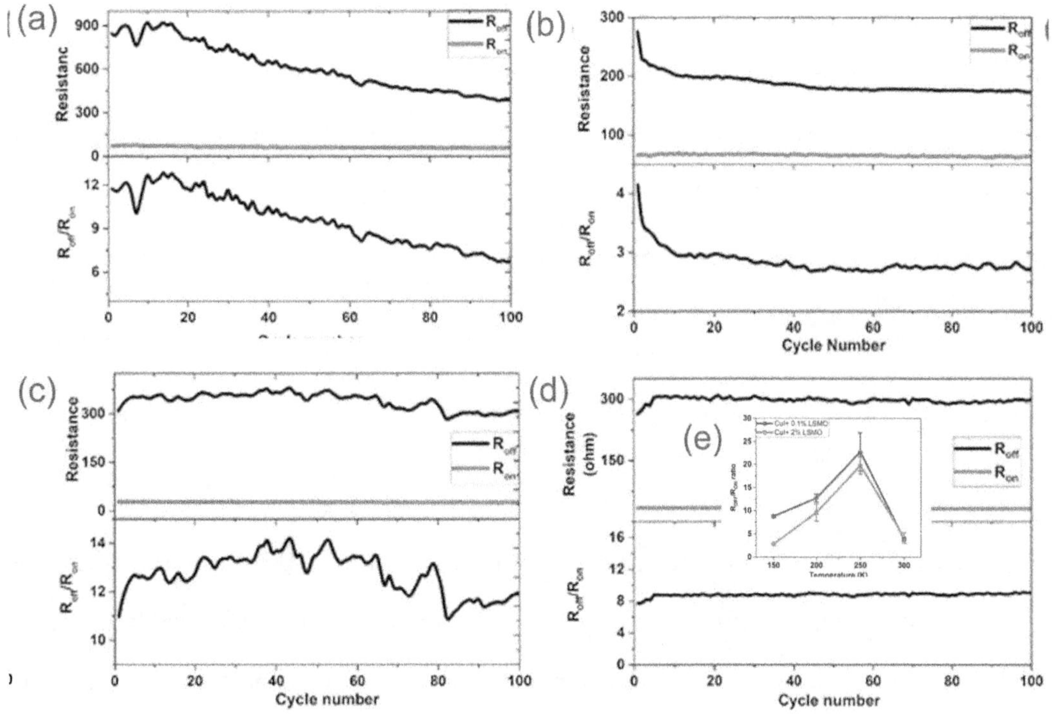

Figure 7.8: R_{on}, R_{off} value for each consecutive cycle for upto 100th cycle for x=0.001 at (a) 250K and (b) 200 K. (c)-(d) represents similar plots for x= 0.02. (e) Variation of averaged ON/OFF ratio over 100 cycles at x= 0.001 and 0.02 for 150 K to 300 K (inset of (d)).

at T= 200K and 150K for x=0.001 average ON/OFF ratio was 9.6 $\pm$1.851 and 2.9 $\pm$ 0.203; and for x=0.02 average ON/OFF ratio was 12.7 $\pm$ 0.853 and 8.8 $\pm$ 0.219 respectively (see Figure. 7.8). We did not observe any specific pattern of rising/diminishing value of ON/OFF ratio as we varied the concentration of LSMO in the nanocomposite. The reason behind the fall in ON/OFF ratio at a temperature lower than 250 K might be associated with the localization of the oxygen ions. As the localized ions lack sufficient thermal energy to cross the barrier or hop from one trapping site to the other. Therefore, the oxygen vacancy sites get partially filled because of reduced migration of oxygen ions which can lead to the reduction in current.

7.3.4 FREQUENCY-DEPENDENT RESISTIVE SWITCHING PROPERTIES

To evaluate the resistive switching properties of the CuI-LSMO nanocomposites, we performed two different sets of pulsed current vs. voltage measurements:

(a) Hysteretic pulse I-V measurement and

(b) Square electrical pulse train I-V measurement.

The origin of the resistive switching and the change in the I-V pattern over cycles can be analyzed from hysteretic pulse I-V measurement. On the other hand, square electrical pulse train I-V measurement can give information about the robustness of the system under a practical switching scenario.

7.3.4.1 CHARACTERISTICS OF THE HYSTERETIC PULSE CURRENT-VOLTAGE MEASUREMENT

The pulsed I-V hysteresis plot of the nanocomposite with x= 0.001 is presented in Figure. 7.9.(a). Hysteresis plots for nanocomposites with x=0.001, 0.005, 0.01, and 0.02 show a switch from high to low resistance state in positive polarity ('Set') and a switch back from low to high resistance state in negative polarity ('Reset'). On the other hand, pristine copper iodide, LSMO and nanocomposite with x = 0.05 did not reveal any sign of resistive switching behavior for the same (see the inset figure of Figure. 7.9.(a)). So overall, the presence of resistive switching behavior in the nanocomposites can be associated with the addition of LSMO.

I-V curve for 1st, 50th, and 100th cycle are presented in Figure. 7.9.(b) for nanocomposites with x=0.001 in a semi-logarithmic scale . Samples retained their memory over repeated switching measurements as there was minimal difference in the I-V plots even after 100 successive cycles. Figure.7.9.(c) and (d) provide the R_{OFF} and R_{ON} values and their ratio for x=0.001 (V_{read}=-0.1 volt) for 100 cycles. The average R_{OFF}/R_{ON} value for x=0.001 was calculated as 10.6 ± 1.2.

7.3.4.2 SWITCHING MECHANISMS

In Figure. 7.9.(e) and (f) we presented the log (I) vs. log(V) plots for positive and negative polarity for the nanocomposite with x=0.001. Here, the 'HRS' region (path '1') of the positive

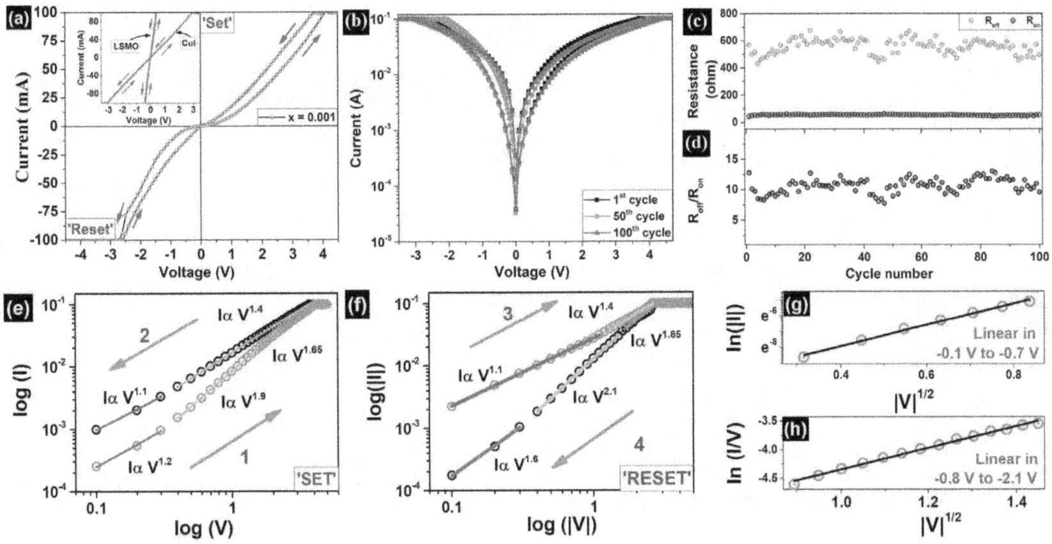

Figure 7.9: (a) Pulsed hysteretic I-V plot of the (1-x)CuI.(x)LSMO nanocomposites with x =0.001. In the inset, hysteresis plot for LSMO and CuI are given. (b) Semi-logarithmic plot of pulsed hysteresic I-V measurement x =0.001 for 1st, 50th and 100th cycle. (c) R_{OFF},R_{ON} value and (d) ON/OFF ratio obtained from the 100 consecutive cycles of pulsed I-V measurement for x =0.001. (e) and (f) represents the log(I) vs. log(V) for positive polarity and negative polarity for x=0.001. (g) ln(I)-$\sqrt{V}$ for SE and (h) ln(I/V)-$\sqrt{V}$ for P-F (for negative polarity) for x =0.001.

polarity/'Set' process (see Figure. 7.9.(e)), can be divided into three sections with slopes of 1.2, 1.9, and 1.65 respectively. Also, the 'HRS' region (path '4') of the negative polarity ('Reset' process, see Figure. 7.9.(f)) can be divided into three sections with slopes 1.6, 2.1, and 1.85 respectively. Here, we noticed that even at the lower bias region in the 'Reset' process, nonlinear conduction behavior is prevalent in contrast to expected ohmic conduction behavior (as observed in the 'Set' process). Now to understand the origin of the nonlinearity in the I-V plot, we have fitted the 'HRS' of the reset process with several conduction mechanisms and among them Schottky mechanism and Poole-Frenkel effect turned out to be the prevalent conduction mechanisms. Now, the relation between current and voltage for Schottky emission and the Poole-Frenkel effect can be reduced in the form of ln(I) vs $\sqrt{V}$ and ln(I/V) vs $\sqrt{V}$ effect respectively.

Now, I-V data of the 'HRS' of the reset process for the x=0.001 is plotted as ln(I) vs. $\sqrt{V}$ and ln(I/V) vs. $\sqrt{V}$ curve which could be linearly fitted in the range of -0.1 volt to -0.7 V and -0.8V to -2.1 V (see Figure. 7.10.(g) and (h)) respectively. In conclusion, Schottky emission dominates the high resistance state initially, rather than the expected ohmic behavior, due to

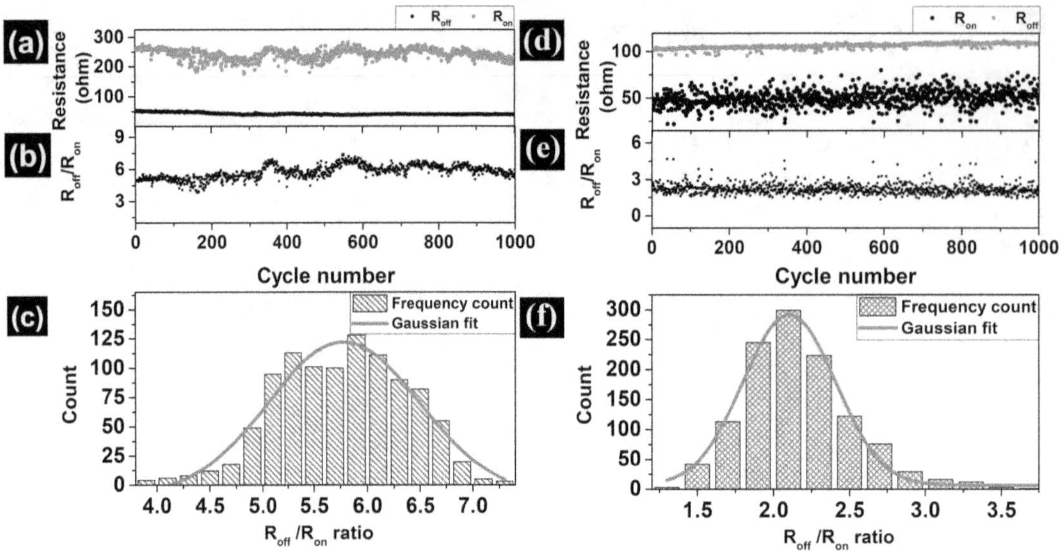

Figure 7.10: R_{OFF}, R_{ON} value obtained from the 1000 consecutive cycle of square electrical pulse train I-V measurement for x=0.001 where pulse width was 100 μs. (b) and (e) R_{OFF}/R_{ON} ratio of the same. (c) and (f) are the frequency distribution of the ON/OFF ratio which is later fitted by the Gaussian distribution.

thermionic emission. This leads to reduced conduction. Poole-Frenkel conduction dominates for V $<$ -0.8 volts, and both mechanisms dominate at different bias voltages of the negative polarity.

7.3.4.3 CHARACTERISTICS OF THE SQUARE ELECTRICAL PULSE TRAIN I-V MEASUREMENT

To investigate the robustness of the resistive switching behavior in a practical scenario, we used square electrical pulse train I-V measurement for 1000 cycles. Two different pulse width of 50 μs and 100 μs were used. Initially, the duty cycle was set to be 20% and 10% but we observed frequent breakdown of the system (i.e HRS state is unable to retain it's resistance state and falling to LRS). Now, when duty cycle was set to 5%, no such breakdown was observed. Also, as 4 data points are required to measure the ON/OFF ratio, the effective frequency of switching was calculated to be 250 Hz and 125 Hz respectively. Therefore, we carried out the experiment with duty cycle of 5% to measure the ON/OFF ratio with V_{read} = -0.1 V. We obtained an average value of 5.8 $\pm$ 0.61 and 2.2 $\pm$ 0.43 (see Figure. 7.10.(a) and (d)) over the span of 1000 cycles for 125 Hz and 250 Hz respectively. To understand the statistical frequency distribution of the R_{OFF}/R_{ON} value, we plotted a histogram plot of the frequency of occurrence of a particular R_{OFF}/R_{ON} value appearing in a cycle and fitted it with Gaussian distribution. Here, we observed that the distribution spanned over a relatively broader range (R_{OFF}/R_{ON} varying from 4.0-7.5) for a frequency of 125 Hz. The distribution range was comparatively shorter for a frequency of 250 Hz (R_{OFF}/R_{ON} varying from 1.5-3.0).

7.4 CONCLUSION

The temperature-dependent resistive switching behavior of (1-x)CuI.(x)LSMO nanocomposites with $0.001<x<0.05$ showed stable RS responses over 100 cycles of hysteretic I-V measurement for all samples. The highest ON/OFF ratio averaged over 100 cycles for x= 0.001 and 0.02 were 19.8 ± 1.85 and 22.7 ± 4.17 respectively (at 250K). From the analysis of the I-V plots, it turned out that Schottky emission and Poole-Frenkel were the dominant conduction mechanism for the low bias and high bias segment of the nonlinear region, respectively. The enhanced switching response of the RS medium after the addition of LSMO can be associated with the oxygen vacancy-induced conduction which was confirmed by XPS. The results above provide insight into how we can alter the resistive switching behavior by adding impurity to the specimen and also how temperature affects the ON/OFF ratio in an RS medium. In the frequency-dependent resistive switching study, RS behavior turned out to be robust over both hysteretic pulse I-V measurement and square electrical pulse train I-V measurement. As we increased the frequency of the switching, the ON/OFF ratio decreased which is expected.

8

CONCLUSION AND SCOPE OF FUTURE WORK

This thesis presents an investigation of multifunctioanl systems based on primarily topological insulators and two-dimensional materials, utilizing a combined theoretical and experimental approach. The experimental section focuses on the characterization of the structures, magnetic and transport properties of these systems, while the theoretical section explores the electronic, magnetic, and transport properties of several 2D materials under the influence of external factors such as strain, doping, and twist angle. The main outcomes of this research are summarized in the current chapter, highlighting the significant findings.

8.1 CONCLUSION

- **Chapter 3**: Structural, magnetic, and transport study of antiferromagnetic topological insulator $MnBi_2Te_4$, $MnBi_4Te_7$, and $Mn_2Bi_2Te_5$
  - **Salient findings**:
    - The layered nature and highly coordinated atomic structures of the samples were observed through scanning electron microscopy and transmission electron microscopy analysis,
    - $MnBi_2Te_4$ exhibited antiferromagnetic behaviour and other two exhibited ferromagnetic coupling. The supposed ferromagnetic behavior observed in some of the samples may be attributed to sample inhomogeneity.
  - **Future scope**:

    * Magnetic, Raman and nonlinear transport measurement of magnetic topological insulators (MTI) under high magnetic field,
    * Exploration of the interplay of magnetism of topology of MTI with other magnetic insulators.

- **Chapter 4**: Effect of interlayer twist on electronic, magnetic, transport, and optical properties of $MnBi_2Te_4/CrGeTe_3$ Van der Walls heterostructure
  - **Salient findings**:
    * With different twist angles between the layers, there were significant changes in the band structure and density of states in the CGT/MBT heterostructure, with only two systems (0° and 10.89°) exhibiting the signature of band inversion.
    * The optical properties of the heterostructure were heavily influenced by the MBT layer, regardless of the twist angle. The exchange coupling between the layers was also estimated using Monte Carlo simulation, and the system was found to be antiferromagnetic at 0° twist angle and ferromagnetic for other angles.
  - **Future scope**:
    * Experimental realization of this theoretical study,
    * Evolution of electronic, magnetic and optical properties of the Van der Walls hetrostructure under gate voltage.

- **Chapter 5**: Proximity induced Colossal Conductivity Modulation in Phosphorene
  - **Salient findings**:
    * Doping, regardless of type, location and concentration, can lead to a significant change in conduction behavior, with a maximum modulation parameter (η) of approximately 570%, particularly with edge doped Sulphur.

    * Applying 2% tensile strain results in a colossal enhancement of current, with a modulation parameter of approximately 1528%.
    * Gate voltage provides a non-invasive means of tuning the effect, with a maximum conduction change of approximately 300% at a gate voltage of 10V.
  - **Future scope**:
    * Experimental realization of this theoretical study,
    * Impact of twist and biaxial strain can offer additional information.

- **Chapter 6**:Strain-controlled operation of Bi_2Se_3 island single electron transistor for chemical sensing and switching applications island
  - **Salient findings**:
    * Doping, regardless of type, location and concentration, can lead to a significant change in conduction behavior, with a maximum modulation parameter (η) of approximately 570%, particularly with edge doped Sulphur.
    * Applying 2% tensile strain results in a colossal enhancement of current, with a modulation parameter of approximately 1528%.
    * Gate voltage provides a non-invasive means of tuning the effect, with a maximum conduction change of approximately 300% at a gate voltage of 10V.
  - **Future scope**:
    * The DFT calculation can be further expanded on few layer Bi_2Se_3
    * Application of biaxial strain can another approach.

- **Chapter 7**: Temperature and frequency-dependent resistive switching properties of copper iodide and $La_{0.7}Sr_{0.3}MnO_3$ based composite systems under various dc and ac excitations.
  - **Salient findings**:

  * The resistive switching (RS) responses of (1-x)CuI.(x)LSMO nanocomposites were stable over 100 repeated cycles of hysteretic I-V measurement for all samples with $0.001<x<0.05$,
  * The dominant conduction mechanisms for the low bias and high bias segments of the nonlinear region were found to be Schottky emission and Poole-Frenkel, respectively,
  * The addition of LSMO enhanced the RS response of the medium, which can be attributed to oxygen vacancy-induced conduction, as confirmed by XPS. The ON/OFF ratio was also found to decrease with increasing frequency of the switching.

- **Future scope**:
  * Investigating the resistive switching characteristics of the composite material following the deposition of a thin film.
  * Impact of external magnetic field on the switching properties.

A

LABVIEW SCRIPTS

Here I have attached the screenshot of the Labview programme I built for the automation of the transport measurement like Current vs Voltage measurement, resistance vs temperature measurement, differential conductance vs voltage at different temperature, Pulse endurance test, Hysteretic current vs Voltage measurement.

I have utilized Keithely 2400, Keithely 2634B, Keithely 6221, Keithely 2182A and Lakeshore 336 temperature controller for this measurements.

(a)

(b)

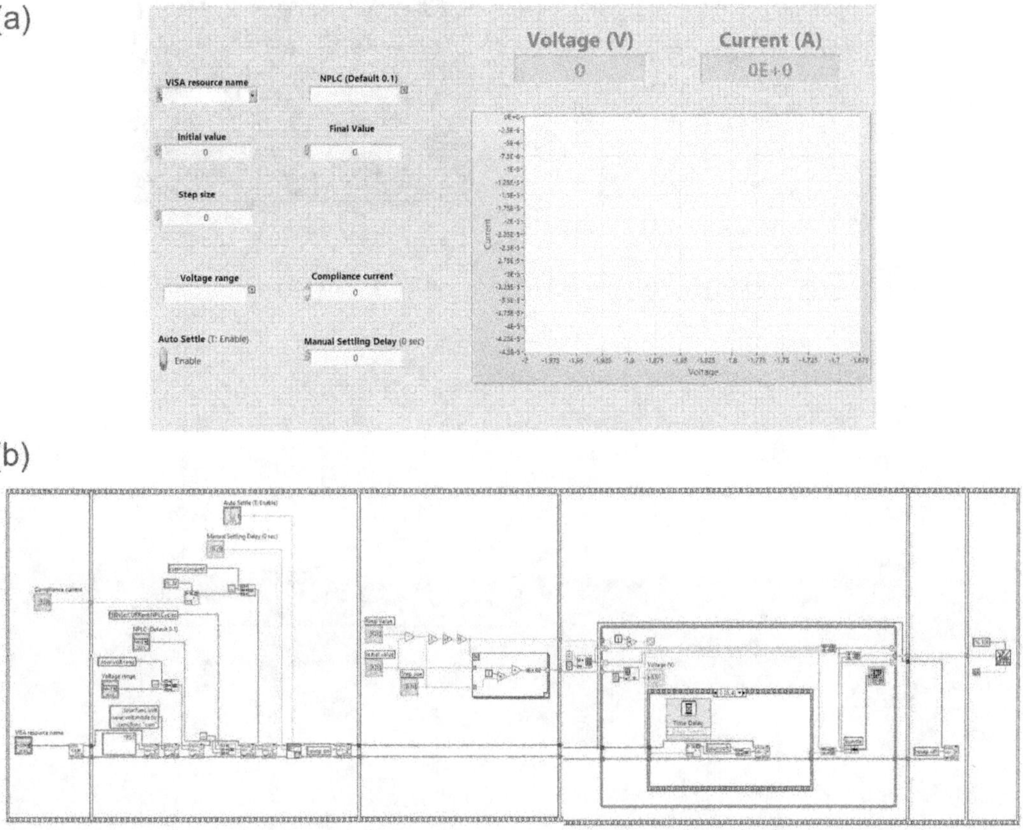

Figure A.1: (a) Current vs Voltage easurement programme made for Keithley 2400 model. (b) Block diagram view of the pragramme.

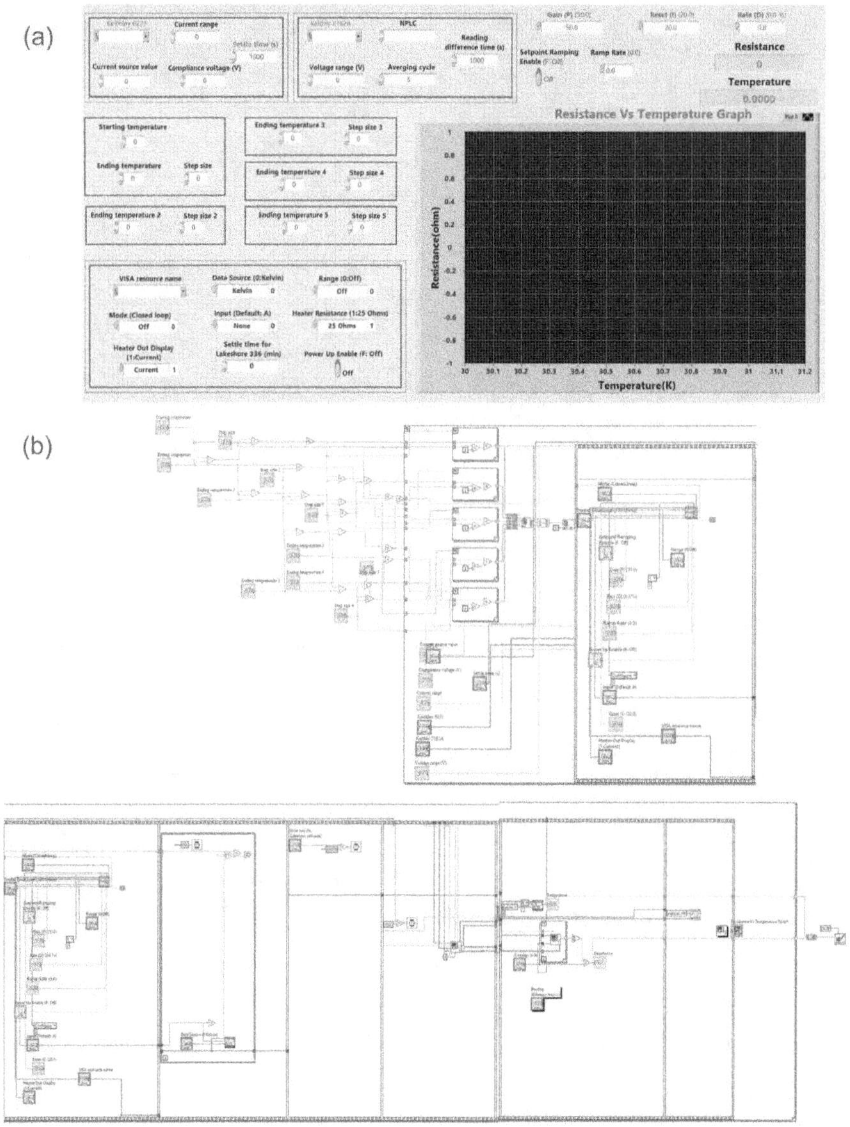

Figure A.2: (a) Front panel of the resistance vs temperature curve programme made for Keithley 6221/2182A and Lakeshore 336 temperature controller. (b)Block diagram view of the pragramme.

BIBLIOGRAPHY

[1] Qing Hua Wang et al. "The Magnetic Genome of Two-Dimensional van der Waals Materials." In: *ACS Nano* 16.5, 2022, pp. 6960–7079.

[2] Abbas Ahmed et al. "Two-dimensional MXenes : New frontier of wearable and flexible electronics." In: *InfoMat* 4.4, 2022,

[3] Pablo Ares et al. "Recent advances in graphene and other 2D materials." In: *Nano Materials Science* 4.1, 2022, pp. 3–9.

[4] Ning Xu et al. "Topological insulators for thermoelectrics." In: *npj Quantum Materials* 2.1, 2017,

[5] Huixia Luo et al. "Topological quantum materials for energy conversion and storage." In: *Nature Reviews Physics* 4.9, 2022, pp. 611–624.

[6] Changhua Bao et al. "Light-induced emergent phenomena in 2D materials and topological materials." In: *Nature Reviews Physics* 4.1, 2021, pp. 33–48.

[7] Noah F. Q. Yuan et al. "Magic of high-order van Hove singularity." In: 10, 2019,

[8] Saquib Shamim et al. "Emergent quantum Hall effects below 50 mT in a two-dimensional topological insulator." In: *Science Advances* 6.26, 2020,

[9] Pawel J. Kowalczyk et al. "Realization of Symmetry-Enforced Two-Dimensional Dirac Fermions in Nonsymmorphic alpha-Bismuthene." In: *ACS Nano* 14.2, 2020, pp. 1888–1894.

[10] K. S. Novoselov et al. "Electric Field Effect in Atomically Thin Carbon Films." In: 306, 2004, pp. 666–669.

[11] N. D. Mermin et al. "Absence of Ferromagnetism or Antiferromagnetism in One- or Two-Dimensional Isotropic Heisenberg Models." In: *Phys. Rev. Lett.* 17, 1966, pp. 1133–1136.

[12] Bevin Huang et al. "Layer-dependent ferromagnetism in a van der Waals crystal down to the monolayer limit." In: *Nature* 546.7657, 2017, pp. 270–273.

[13] Cheng Gong et al. "Discovery of intrinsic ferromagnetism in two-dimensional van der Waals crystals." In: *Nature* 546.7657, 2017, pp. 265–269.

[14] Marco Bianchi et al. "The electronic structure of clean and adsorbate-covered Bi2Te3: an angle-resolved photoemission study." In: *Semiconductor Science and Technology* 27.12, 2012, p. 124001.

[15] Chris Jozwiak et al. "Photoelectron spin-flipping and texture manipulation in a topological insulator." In: *Nature Physics* 9.5, 2013, pp. 293–298.

[16] Anyuan Gao et al. "Layer Hall effect in a 2D topological axion antiferromagnet." In: *Nature* 595.7868, 2021, pp. 521–525.

[17] Shiqi Yang et al. "Odd-Even Layer-Number Effect and Layer-Dependent Magnetic Phase Diagrams in MnBi2Te4." In: *Physical Review X* 11.1, 2021, p. 011003.

[18] Chang Liu et al. "Robust axion insulator and Chern insulator phases in a two-dimensional antiferromagnetic topological insulator." In: *Nature Materials* 19.5, 2020, pp. 522–527.

[19] Haiming Zhu et al. "Interfacial Charge Transfer Circumventing Momentum Mismatch at Two-Dimensional van der Waals Heterojunctions." In: *Nano Letters* 17.6, 2017, pp. 3591–3598.

[20] Kewei Tang et al. "Moiré-Pattern-Tuned Electronic Structures of van der Waals Heterostructures." In: *Advanced Functional Materials* 30.32, 2020, p. 2002672.

[21] Yuan Cao et al. "Unconventional superconductivity in magic-angle graphene superlattices." In: *Nature* 556.7699, 2018, pp. 43–50.

[22] Y. Cao et al. "Superlattice-Induced Insulating States and Valley-Protected Orbits in Twisted Bilayer Graphene." In: 117,

[23] Bing Deng et al. "Interlayer Decoupling in 30° Twisted Bilayer Graphene Quasicrystal." In: *ACS Nano* 14.2, 2020, pp. 1656–1664.

[24] Ke Wu et al. "Identification of twist-angle-dependent excitons in WS2/WSe2 heterobilayers." In: *National Science Review* 9.6, 2021,

[25] Jens Kunstmann et al. "Momentum-space indirect interlayer excitons in transition-metal dichalcogenide van der Waals heterostructures." In: *Nature Physics* 14.8, 2018, pp. 801–805.

[26] Evgeny M. Alexeev et al. "Resonantly hybridized excitons in moiré superlattices in van der Waals heterostructures." In: *Nature* 567.7746, 2019, pp. 81–86.

[27] Arend M. van der Zande et al. "Tailoring the Electronic Structure in Bilayer Molybdenum Disulfide via Interlayer Twist." In: *Nano Letters* 14.7, 2014, pp. 3869–3875.

[28] Kaihui Liu et al. "Evolution of interlayer coupling in twisted molybdenum disulfide bilayers." In: *Nature Communications* 5.1, 2014,

[29] Saptarshi Das et al. "Ambipolar Phosphorene Field Effect Transistor." In: *ACS Nano* 8.11, 2014, pp. 11730–11738.

[30] Rui Cheng et al. "Few-layer molybdenum disulfide transistors and circuits for high-speed flexible electronics." In: *Nature Communications* 5.1, 2014,

[31] K. S. Novoselov et al. "2D materials and van der Waals heterostructures." In: *Science* 353.6298, 2016,

[32] Junyong Wang et al. "Electroluminescent Devices Based on 2D Semiconducting Transition Metal Dichalcogenides." In: *Advanced Materials* 30.47, 2018, p. 1802687.

[33] Nengjie Huo et al. "Photoresponsive and Gas Sensing Field-Effect Transistors based on Multilayer WS2 Nanoflakes." In: *Scientific Reports* 4.1, 2014,

[34] Jongyeol Baek et al. "A highly sensitive chemical gas detecting transistor based on highly crystalline CVD-grown MoSe2 films." In: *Nano Research* 10.6, 2016, pp. 1861–1871.

[35] Shiqi Guo et al. "Development of a Cloud-Based Epidermal MoSe2 Device for Hazardous Gas Sensing." In: *Advanced Functional Materials* 29.18, 2019, p. 1900138.

[36] Rui Cheng et al. "Electroluminescence and Photocurrent Generation from Atomically Sharp WSe2/MoS2 Heterojunction p-n Diodes." In: *Nano Letters* 14.10, 2014, pp. 5590–5597.

[37] Yexin Deng et al. "Black Phosphorus-Monolayer MoS2 van der Waals Heterojunction p-n Diode." In: *ACS Nano* 8.8, 2014, pp. 8292–8299.

[38] Feng Wang et al. "Tunable GaTe-MoS2 van der Waals p-n Junctions with Novel Optoelectronic Performance." In: *Nano Letters* 15.11, 2015, pp. 7558–7566.

[39] R. S. Sundaram et al. "Electroluminescence in Single Layer MoS2." In: *Nano Letters* 13.4, 2013, pp. 1416–1421.

[40] C. Stampfer et al. "Tunable Graphene Single Electron Transistor." In: *Nano Letters* 8.8, 2008, pp. 2378–2383.

[41] Wenhui Niu et al. "Exceptionally clean single-electron transistors from solutions of molecular graphene nanoribbons." In: *Nature Materials* 22.2, 2023, pp. 180–185.

[42] Kyunghoon Lee et al. "Coulomb blockade in monolayer MoS2 single electron transistor." In: *Nanoscale* 8.14, 2016, pp. 7755–7760.

[43] Salisu Nasir et al. "Potential valorization of by-product materials from oil palm: A review of alternative and sustainable carbon sources for carbon-based nanomaterials synthesis." In: *BioResources* 14.1, 2019,

[44] Katsuhiko Inaba et al. "High Resolution X-Ray Diffraction Analyses of (La,Sr)MnO3/ZnO/Sapphire(0001) Double Heteroepitaxial Films." In: *Advances in Materials Physics and Chemistry* 03.01, 2013, pp. 72–89.

[45] "https://ravescientific.com/products/high-resolution-fesem-zeiss-sigma." In:

[46] "https://www.vcbio.science.ru.nl/en/fesem/eds/." In:

[47] W. Kohn et al. "Self-Consistent Equations Including Exchange and Correlation Effects." In: *Physical Review* 140.4A, 1965, A1133–A1138.

[48] P. Hohenberg et al. In: *Physical Review* 136.3B, 1964, B864–B871.

[49] John P. Perdew et al. In: *Physical Review B* 46.11, 1992, pp. 6671–6687.

[50] John P. Perdew et al. In: *Physical Review B* 33.12, 1986, pp. 8800–8802.

[51] R. Landauer. "Spatial variation of currents and fields due to localized scatterers in metallic conduction." In: *IBM Journal of Research and Development* 32.3, 1988, pp. 306–316.

[52] M. Büttiker et al. "Generalized many-channel conductance formula with application to small rings." In: *Phys. Rev. B* 31, 10 1985, pp. 6207–6215.

[53] J.-Q. Yan et al. "Crystal growth and magnetic structure of MnBi2Te4." In: *Physical Review Materials* 3.6, 2019, p. 064202.

[54] Lei Ding et al. "Crystal and magnetic structures of magnetic topological insulators MnBi2Te4 and MnBi 4Te7." In: *Physical Review B* 101.2, 2020, p. 020412.

[55] A. K. Geim et al. "Van der Waals heterostructures." In: 499, 2013, pp. 419–425.

[56] Elad Koren et al. "Coherent commensurate electronic states at the interface between misoriented graphene layers." In: *Nature Nanotechnology* 11.9, 2016, pp. 752–757.

[57] A. Chaudhury et al. "Proximity-Induced Colossal Conductivity Modulation in Phosphorene." In: *Physical Review Applied* 11.2, 2019, p. 024056.

[58] P. Kumari et al. "High efficiency spin filtering in magnetic phosphorene." In: *Physical Chemistry Chemical Physics* 22.10, 2020, pp. 5893–5901.

[59] S. Kar et al. "Stimuli assisted electronic, magnetic and optical phase control in CrOBr monolayer." In: *Physica E: Low-dimensional Systems and Nanostructures* 143, 2022, p. 115332.

[60] Matthew Yankowitz et al. "Tuning superconductivity in twisted bilayer graphene." In: *Science* 363.6431, 2019, pp. 1059–1064.

[61] Zhen Bi et al. "Designing flat bands by strain." In: *Physical Review B* 100.3, 2019, p. 035448.

[62] Shuai Zhang et al. "Abnormal conductivity in low-angle twisted bilayer graphene." In: 6, 2020,

[63] Kyounghwan Kim et al. "Tunable moiré bands and strong correlations in small-twist-angle bilayer graphene." In: *Proceedings of the National Academy of Sciences* 114.13, 2017, pp. 3364–3369.

[64] Wen-Yu He et al. "Giant orbital magnetoelectric effect and current-induced magnetization switching in twisted bilayer graphene." In: *Nature Communications* 11.1, 2020,

[65] M. Serlin et al. "Intrinsic quantized anomalous Hall effect in a moire heterostructure." In: *Science* 367.6480, 2020, pp. 900–903.

[66] Trithep Devakul et al. "Magic in twisted transition metal dichalcogenide bilayers." In: *Nature Communications* 12.1, 2021,

[67] Kha Tran et al. "Evidence for moire excitons in van der Waals heterostructures." In: *Nature* 567.7746, 2019, pp. 71–75.

[68] Chenhao Jin et al. "Observation of moire excitons in WSe2/WS2 heterostructure superlattices." In: *Nature* 567.7746, 2019, pp. 76–80.

[69] Matthew R. Rosenberger et al. "Twist Angle-Dependent Atomic Reconstruction and Moiré Patterns in Transition Metal Dichalcogenide Heterostructures." In: *ACS Nano* 14.4, 2020, pp. 4550–4558.

[70] Soumya Sarkar et al. "Direct Bandgap-like Strong Photoluminescence from Twisted Multilayer MoS2 Grown on SrTiO3." In: 14, 2020, pp. 16761–16769.

[71] Shengxi Huang et al. "Probing the Interlayer Coupling of Twisted Bilayer MoS2 Using Photoluminescence Spectroscopy." In: *Nano Letters* 14.10, 2014, pp. 5500–5508.

[72] Matheus I. N. Rosa et al. "Topological gaps by twisting." In: *Communications Physics* 4.1, 2021,

[73] Jue Wang et al. "Optical generation of high carrier densities in 2D semiconductor heterobilayers." In: *Science Advances* 5.9, 2019,

[74] Kyle L. Seyler et al. "Signatures of moiré-trapped valley excitons in MoSe2/WSe2 heterobilayers." In: *Nature* 567.7746, 2019, pp. 66–70.

[75] Qingjun Tong et al. "Skyrmions in the Moiré of van der Waals 2D Magnets." In: *Nano Letters* 18.11, 2018, pp. 7194–7199.

[76] Kasra Hejazi et al. "Heterobilayer moiré magnets: Moiré skyrmions and commensurate-incommensurate transitions." In: *Physical Review B* 104.10, 2021, p. 1100406.

[77] Chong Wang et al. "Stacking Domain Wall Magnons in Twisted van der Waals Magnets." In: *Physical Review Letters* 125.24, 2020, p. 247201.

[78] Kasra Hejazi et al. "Noncollinear phases in moire magnets." In: *Proceedings of the National Academy of Sciences* 117.20, 2020, pp. 10721–10726.

[79] Nikhil Sivadas et al. "Stacking-Dependent Magnetism in Bilayer CrI3." In: *Nano Letters* 18.12, 2018, pp. 7658–7664.

[80] Tingxin Li et al. "Pressure-controlled interlayer magnetism in atomically thin CrI3." In: *Nature Materials* 18.12, 2019, pp. 1303–1308.

[81] Tiancheng Song et al. "Switching 2D magnetic states via pressure tuning of layer stacking." In: *Nature Materials* 18.12, 2019, pp. 1298–1302.

[82] Haowei Peng et al. "Rehabilitation of the Perdew-Burke-Ernzerhof generalized gradient approximation for layered materials." In: *Physical Review B* 95.8, 2017, p. 081105.

[83] Haowei Peng et al. "Versatile van der Waals Density Functional Based on a Meta-Generalized Gradient Approximation." In: *Physical Review X* 6.4, 2016, p. 041005.

[84] Huixia Fu et al. "Exchange bias and quantum anomalous Hall effect in the MnBi2Te4 /CrI3 heterostructure." In: 6, 2020,

[85] Kangying Wang et al. "Magnetic and electronic properties of Cr3 monolayer by strain and electric-field engineering." In: *Applied Physics Letters* 114.9, 2019, p. 092405.

[86] Jiaheng Li et al. "Intrinsic magnetic topological insulators in van der Waals layered MnBi2Te4 -family materials." In: *Science Advances* 5.6, 2019,

[87] Chi Xuan Trang et al. "Crossover from 2D Ferromagnetic Insulator to Wide Band Gap Quantum Anomalous Hall Insulator in Ultrathin MnBi2Te4." In: *ACS Nano* 15.8, 2021, pp. 13444–13452.

[88] Yuanyue Liu et al. "Two-Dimensional Mono-Elemental Semiconductor with Electronically Inactive Defects: The Case of Phosphorus." In: *Nano Letters* 14.12, 2014, PMID: 25162380, pp. 6782–6786. eprint: http://dx.doi.org/10.1021/nl5021393. URL: http://dx.doi.org/10.1021/nl5021393.

[89] Zhen Zhu et al. "Semiconducting Layered Blue Phosphorus: A Computational Study." In: *Phys. Rev. Lett.* 112, 17 2014, p. 176802.

[90] Hongyan Guo et al. "Phosphorene Nanoribbons, Phosphorus Nanotubes, and van der Waals Multilayers." In: *The Journal of Physical Chemistry C* 118.25, 2014, pp. 14051–14059.

[91] Jiayu Dai et al. "Gas adsorption on graphene doped with B, N, Al, and S: A theoretical study." In: *Applied Physics Letters* 95.23, 232105, 2009,

[92] A. N. Rudenko et al. "Quasiparticle band structure and tight-binding model for single- and bilayer black phosphorus." In: *Phys. Rev. B* 89, 20 2014, p. 201408. URL: https://link.aps.org/doi/10.1103/PhysRevB.89.201408.

[93] Ahmet Avsar et al. "Gate-tunable black phosphorus spin valve with nanosecond spin lifetimes." In: *Nature Physics* 13, May 2017, 888 EP.

[94] Likai Li et al. "Black Phosphorus Field-effect Transistors." In: *Nature Nanotechnology* 9.5, May 2014, pp. 372–377.

[95] Ruixiang Fei et al. "Strain-Engineering the Anisotropic Electrical Conductance of Few-Layer Black Phosphorus." In: *Nano Letters* 14.5, 2014, pp. 2884–2889.

[96] S. J. Ray et al. "Unconventional strain-dependent conductance oscillations in pristine phosphorene." In: *Phys. Chem. Chem. Phys.* 20, 19 2018, pp. 13508–13516.

[97] Gen Long et al. "Achieving Ultrahigh Carrier Mobility in Two-Dimensional Hole Gas of Black Phosphorus." In: *Nano Letters* 16.12, 2016, pp. 7768–7773.

[98] F. Schedin et al. "Detection of Individual Gas Molecules adsorbed on Graphene." In: *Nat Mater* 6.9, Sept. 2007, pp. 652–655.

[99] S. Rani et al. "Detection of gas molecule using C3N island single electron transistor." In: *Carbon* 144, 2019, pp. 235 –240.

[100] Yuehua Xu et al. "Electron-Transport Properties of Few-Layer Black Phosphorus." In: *The Journal of Physical Chemistry Letters* 6.11, 2015, pp. 1996–2002.

[101] Ajanta Maity et al. "Structural, electronic, mechanical, and transport properties of phosphorene nanoribbons: Negative differential resistance behavior." In: *Phys. Rev. B* 94, 7 2016, p. 075422.

[102] R. Chowdhury et al. "Graphene-based biosensor using transport properties." In: *Physical Review B* 83.4, 2011, p. 045401.

[103] Qingyun Wu et al. "Electronic and transport properties of phosphorene nanoribbons." In: *Phys. Rev. B* 92, 3 2015, p. 035436.

[104] V. Hung Nguyen et al. "Giant effect of negative differential conductance in graphene nanoribbon p-n hetero-junctions." In: *Applied Physics Letters* 99.4, 2011, p. 042105.

[105] Xuesong Li et al. "Large-Area Synthesis of High-Quality and Uniform Graphene Films on Copper Foils." In: *Science* 324.5932, 2009, pp. 1312–1314.

[106] P. Sutter et al. "Interface Formation in Monolayer Graphene-Boron Nitride Heterostructures." In: *Nano Letters* 12.9, 2012, pp. 4869–4874.

[107] Zheng Liu et al. "Direct Growth of Graphene/Hexagonal Boron Nitride Stacked Layers." In: *Nano Letters* 11.5, 2011, pp. 2032–2037.

[108] Anchal Srivastava et al. "Novel Liquid Precursor-Based Facile Synthesis of Large-Area Continuous, Single, and Few-Layer Graphene Films." In: *Chemistry of Materials* 22.11, 2010, pp. 3457–3461.

[109] César Moreno et al. "Bottom-up synthesis of multifunctional nanoporous graphene." In: *Science* 360.6385, 2018, pp. 199–203.

[110] Maxim Ziatdinov et al. "Visualization of electronic states on atomically smooth graphitic edges with different types of hydrogen termination." In: *Phys. Rev. B* 87, 11 2013, p. 115427.

[111] Levente Tapasztó et al. "Tailoring the atomic structure of graphene nanoribbons by scanning tunnelling microscope lithography." In: *Nature Nanotechnology* 3, June 2008, 397 EP –.

[112] Brett R. Goldsmith et al. "Conductance-Controlled Point Functionalization of Single-Walled Carbon Nanotubes." In: *Science* 315.5808, 2007, pp. 77–81.

[113] Saptarshi Das et al. "Screening and interlayer coupling in multilayer MoS2." In: *physica status solidi (RRL) - Rapid Research Letters* 7.4, 2013, pp. 268–273.

[114] Saptarshi Das et al. "Where Does the Current Flow in Two-Dimensional Layered Systems?" In: *Nano Letters* 13.7, 2013, pp. 3396–3402.

[115] Serge Luryi. "Quantum capacitance devices." In: *Applied Physics Letters* 52.6, 1988, pp. 501–503.

[116] Tian Tian et al. "Multiscale Analysis for Field-Effect Penetration through Two-Dimensional Materials." In: *Nano Letters* 16.8, 2016, pp. 5044–5052.

[117] Sungjae Cho et al. "Topological Insulator Quantum Dot with Tunable Barriers." In: *Nano Letters* 12.1, 2011, pp. 469–472.

[118] Yumei Jing et al. "A Single-Electron Transistor Made of a 3D Topological Insulator Nanoplate." In: *Advanced Materials* 31.42, 2019, p. 1903686.

[119] Mads Brandbyge et al. "Density-functional method for nonequilibrium electron transport." In: *Physical Review B* 65.16, 2002, p. 165401.

[120] Jeremy Taylor et al. "Ab initiomodeling of quantum transport properties of molecular electronic devices." In: *Physical Review B* 63.24, 2001, p. 245407.

[121] P.M Sirimanne et al. "Characterization of transparent conducting CuI thin films prepared by pulse laser deposition technique." In: *Chemical Physics Letters* 366.5-6, 2002, pp. 485–489.

[122] N. P. Klochko et al. "Solution-produced copper iodide thin films for photosensor and for vertical thermoelectric nanogenerator, which uses a spontaneous temperature gradient." In: *Journal of Materials Science: Materials in Electronics* 30.18, 2019, pp. 17514–17524.

[123] J.-H. Park et al. "Magnetic Properties at Surface Boundary of a Half-Metallic FerromagnetLa0.7Sr0.3MnO3." In: *Physical Review Letters* 81.9, 1998, pp. 1953–1956.

[124] Nabil Kallel et al. "Magnetocaloric properties in the Cr-doped La0.7Sr0.3MnO3 manganites." In: *Physica B: Condensed Matter* 404.2, 2009, pp. 285–288.

[125] Rainer Waser et al. "Introduction to new memory paradigms: memristive phenomena and neuromorphic applications." In: *Faraday Discussions* 213, 2019, pp. 11–27.

[126] Liyu Peng et al. "Reduction in thermal conductivity of Sb2Te phase-change material by scandium/yttrium doping." In: *Journal of Alloys and Compounds* 821, 2020, p. 153499.

[127] Andrew D. Kent et al. "A new spin on magnetic memories." In: *Nature Nanotechnology* 10.3, 2015, pp. 187–191.

[128] Huitao Shen et al. "In-Plane Ferroelectric Tunnel Junction." In: *Physical Review Applied* 11.2, 2019, p. 024048.

[129] Chun-An Lin et al. "Impact of barrier layer on HfO2-based conductive bridge random access memory." In: *Applied Physics Letters* 114.9, 2019, p. 093105.

[130] Kyungho Hong et al. "Investigation of the Thermal Recovery From Reset Breakdown of a SiN x -Based RRAM." In: *IEEE Transactions on Electron Devices* 67.4, 2020, pp. 1600–1605.

[131] Karl-Magnus Persson et al. "Cross-Point Arrays with Low-Power ITO-HfO 2 Resistive Memory Cells Integrated on Vertical III-V Nanowires." In: *Advanced Electronic Materials* 6.6, 2020, p. 2000154.

[132] Botond Sánta et al. "Nanosecond resistive switching in Ag/AgI/PtIr nanojunctions." In: *Beilstein Journal of Nanotechnology* 11, 2020, pp. 92–100.

[133] G. Zisis et al. "Enhanced electro-optic response in domain-engineered LiNbO3 channel waveguides." In: *Applied Physics Letters* 109.2, 2016, p. 021101.

[134] Xiangxiang Ding et al. "Low-Power Resistive Switching Characteristic in HfO2/TiOx Bi-Layer Resistive Random-Access Memory." In: *Nanoscale Research Letters* 14.1, 2019,

[135] Deok-Hwang Kwon et al. "Unraveling the Origin and Mechanism of Nanofilament Formation in Polycrystalline SrTiO 3 Resistive Switching Memories." In: *Advanced Materials* 31.28, 2019, p. 1901322.

[136] Y. B. Lin et al. "Temperature-dependent and polarization-tuned resistive switching in Au/BiFeO3/SrRuO3 junctions." In: *Applied Physics Letters* 104.14, 2014, p. 143503.

[137] Chandreswar Mahata et al. "Resistive switching and synaptic behaviors of an HfO2/Al2O3 stack on ITO for neuromorphic systems." In: *Journal of Alloys and Compounds* 826, 2020, p. 154434.

[138] Hehe Zhang et al. "Understanding the Coexistence of Two Bipolar Resistive Switching Modes with Opposite Polarity in Pt/TiO2/Ti/Pt Nanosized ReRAM Devices." In: *ACS Applied Materials & Interfaces* 10.35, 2018, pp. 29766–29778.

[139] Niloufar Raeis-Hosseini et al. "Resistive switching memory using biomaterials." In: 39, 2017, pp. 223–238.

[140] Shantanu Majumder et al. "Pulsed voltage induced resistive switching behavior of copper iodide and La0.7Sr0.3MnO3 nanocomposites." In: *Materials Letters* 302, 2021, p. 130339.

[141] Elke Beyreuther et al. "XPS investigation of Mn valence in lanthanum manganite thin films under variation of oxygen content." In: *Physical Review B* 73.15, 2006, p. 155425.

[142] Rajasree Das et al. "Multiferroic properties of Ba2+and Gd3+co-doped bismuth ferrite: magnetic, ferroelectric and impedance spectroscopic analysis." In: 45, 2012, p. 455002.

[143] Mark T. Greiner et al. "Transition Metal Oxide Work Functions: The Influence of Cation Oxidation State and Oxygen Vacancies." In: *Advanced Functional Materials* 22.21, 2012, pp. 4557–4568.

www.ingramcontent.com/pod-product-compliance
Lightning Source LLC
LaVergne TN
LVHW082347200926
848481LV00012B/3488